Senate Prayers

AND

SPIRES OF THE SPIRIT

Senate Prayers

AND

SPIRES OF THE SPIRIT

FREDERICK BROWN HARRIS

edited by J. D. Phelan

THE BETHANY PRESS

ST. LOUIS, MISSOURI

All of the "Spires of the Spirit" are reprinted, with editorial changes, from the *Washington Star*. The following were copyrighted by the *Washington Star*:

"The Need for Uncommon Common Men," copyright 1964; "The Curtain of Light," copyright 1965; "A Glorious Gift to Liberty," copyright 1967; "The Man in the Mirror," copyright 1968; "If He Had Not Come," copyright 1966; "Everybody's Saint," copyright 1965.

Used by permission.

Slight editorial changes were made in the prayers, which first appeared in the *Congressional Record*.

Stanza 4, "God of Grace and God of Glory" by Harry Emerson Fosdick, p. 33, used by permission of Elinor Fosdick Downs.

Verses from "Sanctuary" by John Oxenham, pp. 40, 145, used by permission of Theo Oxenham.

Lines from "He Was a Gambler Too" by G. A. Studdert-Kennedy, p. 72, reprinted from *The Unutterable Beauty* by G. A. Studdert-Kennedy by permission of Hodder and Stoughton Ltd.

Poetry, p. 103, from "Renascence" by Edna St. Vincent Millay. *Collected Poems*, Harper & Row. Copyright 1917, 1945 by Edna St. Vincent Millay. By permission of Norma Millay Ellis.

Scripture quotations, unless otherwise noted, are from the *Revised Standard Version of the Bible*, copyrighted 1946 and 1952 by the Division of Christian Education, National Council of Churches of Christ in the United States of America, and used by permission.

Distributed by The G. R. Welch Company, Toronto, Ontario, Canada. Other foreign distribution by Feffer and Simons, Inc., New York, New York.

MANUFACTURED IN THE UNITED STATES OF AMERICA

To my wife
         Helen

Quietly in loving praise
   She let me know in gentle ways
Her never-failing faith.
   How often I would search
      a crowd to find her face,
      as her resplendent glance
      worked its alchemy.

So hear this grateful prayer
   "That shall upbear
   The incense of my thankfulness
   For this sweet grace
      of Warmth and Light."

THE WHITE HOUSE

WASHINGTON

March 22, 1970

Dear Dr. Harris:

How good it was to hear from you and to learn of
your intention to publish a volume containing a
number of the Senate prayers and a collection of
your weekly column, "Spires of the Spirit."

For many years your words brought inspiration,
encouragement and strength to our legislative
leaders. Those of us who knew you and bene-
fited from your Chaplaincy are particularly
gratified to know that your statements will live
on to enrich future generations of Americans.

Mrs. Nixon joins me in sending you our kindest
regards and warm best wishes always.

Sincerely,

Richard Nixon

Reverend Frederick Brown Harris
The Westchester
4000 Cathedral Avenue, NW.
Washington, D.C. 20016

SENATE PRAYERS

Contents

Foreword

"GOD LOVE THAT MAN!" These words came to my ears from a young mother who, with her husband and two little children, was seated on a deacon's bench in back of Mrs. Wells and me when we dedicated the Faith of Our Fathers Chapel at Valley Forge on Sunday, April 30, 1967. These heartfelt words of gratitude were for Dr. Frederick Brown Harris—the late distinguished American literary leader and spiritual guide.

"No man wearing the cloth of the clergy has more influentially illuminated the purposes and the aspirations of our country than my good friend Dr. Harris, for nearly a quarter of a century chaplain of the U. S. Senate"—so said his friend General Dwight D. Eisenhower at a meeting of the national Board of Trustees of Freedoms Foundation at Valley Forge the first week in December, 1967.

"To me, Reverend Harris is the anchor man on the American spiritual team," said Rabbi Norman Gerstenfeld of the Washington Hebrew Congregation, while standing with other distinguished leaders having their picture taken in the old Senate Supreme Court Chambers, when Freedoms Foundation awards were being presented.

Accolades from the high and mighty, and the warmly reciprocated love of parents and little children, came from all points of the compass. I thrilled at receiving a handwritten letter from Chaplain Fred—the jubilant, searching scholar—the young man from Dickinson College—the fair, outspoken, gentle, penetrating pastor for forty years at Foundry Methodist Church in Washington. This beloved, gracious man deserved recognition for service so impelling to all the human family he touched.

His joy was with Helen, his wise and attractive "bride" through the many years, who was devoted and faithful to every task he undertook. Where, oh where, is another with the grace and talents of Helen?

Yes, Fred Harris—buoyant public leader, committed man of God, most desired of companions—served with love and practical common sense. His words were ever words of hope in treasured phrases for all who ever knew him, whether in pain, in joy, or in search of life's profound meanings. Fred Harris— minister to presidents, senators, people from the bench, from the machine, the ticket counter, and the farm—was every man's inspiration.

For half a century he turned his face and heart toward the Sermon on the Mount and his feet to the spiritual needs of mankind. And to the time of his death—August 18, 1970— he served the cause of freedom because he served the cause of men as children of God.

KENNETH D. WELLS
President, Freedoms Foundation
Valley Forge, Pennsylvania

≽ 1 ≼

OUR FATHER, who putteth down the mighty from their seat and exalteth the humble and the meek, thou to whom a thousand years are but as one day, while life's ebbing hours last make us bold and swift to find and do thy will for our times. In all the fever and fret of a confused day, may we never forget that he that is slow to anger is better than the mighty, and he that ruleth his own heart is better than he that taketh a city.

In this exalted chamber of governance, we beseech thee, pour the riches of thy grace upon those who here stand in the nation's name: upon the president of the Republic, who this day upon the Holy Bible, the charter of our costly freedom, takes again the oath of his great office; upon the vice-president; and upon the Congress. Pour for these momentous times a double portion of thy Spirit.

Save us from lowering the shield of national unity and solidarity in a perilous hour when the poisonous arrows of tyranny are being aimed by determined foes at the very life of this dear land of our hope and prayer. To all who serve in the ministry of public affairs give fairness of appraisal, poise amid confusion, a kindly heart, nobility of goodness, and a simple faith in man that is more than coronets.

We ask it in the Name that is above every name. *Amen.*

≽ 2 ≼

ETERNAL FATHER, strong to save, all that we think or plan or do this sacred week has upon it the shadow of a rugged cross. With a surety that pure reason cannot follow, because it passeth understanding, we are conscious that in the face of Christ, man's best man, love's best love, as he moves with unshrinking, steady pace to the cross-crowned hill outside the city's walls, is the confirmation of our highest aspirations, the rebuke to our failure to be true to our best, the shining goal of a self uncowed by the threats of foes or compromised by the seduction of friends.

> I take, O cross, thy shadow
>   For my abiding place;
> I ask no other sunshine than
>   The sunshine of his face;
> Content to let the world go by,
>   To know no gain nor loss,
> My sinful self my only shame,
>   My glory all the cross.

In Jesus' name, who for the joy that was set before him endured the cross and despised the shame. *Amen.*

3

OUR FATHER, who standeth sure amid the shifting sands of time, like men who turn from dusty toil to crystal streams, we lift our soiled faces to thee, from the perplexities and imperfections that crowd our days and drain our powers of endurance. In conscience, in quiet moments when above earth's strident voices the still, small voice speaks to our inmost self, in soaring thoughts that will not stay on the ground, in deep needs that drive us to thee, in the sacrament of human love, in the beauty of nature, and in the spiritual heritage of our race through seers and prophets and, above all, Christ, thou dost stand at the door and knock.

Give us, we pray thee, the grace of hospitality to the highest and the best. Because there is no solution to the world's ills, except as it springs from the hearts of men, we pray for ourselves: Cleanse thou our hearts by thy grace, feed our minds with thy truth, guide our feet in the paths of righteousness, for thy Name's sake. *Amen.*

❧ 4 ❧

O GOD of grace and glory, in whose love and wisdom lie all our help and hope, in these hectic and explosive days may we be strengthened with might and our jaded souls refreshed as thou dost lead us into green pastures and beside still waters.

> Spirit of purity and grace,
> Our weakness pitying see,
> O make our hearts thy dwelling place,
> And worthier of thee.

Amen.

❧ 5 ❧

O GOD, before whom our little span of years is like the brief shining of a candle, while it yet burns we would yield our flickering torch to thee so that in thine hands the flame of our lives may be part of the light that glows in the darkness.

Thou hast made this earth so fair and given it to all men to enjoy richly. Help us never to grow dull to all its wonders or lose the mystic luster of the changing pageant of earth and sky and sea. Above all, may no blighting acids of disillusionment or cynicism blind us to the glory of our common humanity as the splendor of it flames in the warmth of human fellowship, in the sacrament of love and friendship, in the trusting innocence of adorable children, and even in the weak, who need the buttressing of our belief in them, and in the strong, who give us of their strength. We thank thee for dauntless souls who, in spite of persecution, postponement, and bitter cost, have followed the gleam of brighter and better days.

Join us to the seers and prophets of the past who have gone ahead of the crowd to climb the beckoning hilltops of humanity's highest hopes.

In the dear Redeemer's name. *Amen.*

⚜ 6 ⚜

OUR FATHER, author of liberty, out of historic yesterdays we are conscious of a cloud of witnesses whose peering eyes are upon us. As a grateful nation prepared to hallow its yesterdays and to remember the cost of its liberties—freedoms that are threatened now as never before by sinister forces that deal in tyranny and chains—we are asking for help to realize that our glorious heritage is not like an ancient heirloom from the past that can be handed down to generations following, but a spiritual thing that must be reinterpreted, relived, and rewon with every new test that the changing years bring.

Today beneath the great white dome, which in its illuminated majesty is a symbol to the nation of the American dream, there rest, in honor, on the journey to the Tomb of the Unknown, representatives of those who gave their lives so that their mortal bodies might be shields to defend our freedom. May the rotunda, mecca for millions, be a vast, whispering gallery where, for multitudes of pilgrims, a voice may be heard: "It was for visions we fell." Stir our hearts with the beauty of that vision which by faith is brought near when—

Nation with nation, land with land
Unarmed shall live as comrades free;
In every heart and brain shall throb
The pulse of one fraternity.

In the name of that Holy One whose truth shall make all men free. *Amen.*

❧ 7 ❧

OUR FATHER, we thank thee for the sweet refreshment of sleep, restoring the frayed edges of care, and for fresh vigor to meet the new day.

Across all its toiling hours, O thou Great Companion of our pilgrim way, keep our hearts with thee, as once more those who here speak and act for the nation face vexing national and global problems which tax their utmost to solve.

While they heed the judgments of those who share with them the responsibilities of statecraft, teach them to test all things by their own consciences and by the teachings and Spirit of the one who alone is our Master.

Strengthen our every weakness; calm our anxieties; control our ill tempers. Save us from fear and cynicism; make us worthy of these demanding times, which try men's souls and cry aloud for wisdom and character.

We ask it in the dear Redeemer's name. *Amen.*

❧ 8 ❧

OUR GOD, in this shrine of each patriot's devotion, for toiling months a few out of the millions have been allowed by thee to be servants of the nation in a tense and tortured time when the earth has been plowed with violence, when brave fighters for freedom have been met and subdued by the bayonets of tyrants, and when wars and rumors of war have vexed the world.

In such a day, thou hast summoned us to strengthen the bulwarks of liberty and to mobilize the might of freedom against malignant, rampant evil bent on enslaving all peoples.

Now that the sands of this session of deliberations have almost run out, we acknowledge that at best we have been but unprofitable servants.

Now unto thy holy keeping we commit ourselves and the nation, as on the last page of another national volume is about to be inscribed, "What we have written, we have written."

Bless and strengthen all that here has been done worthily, as the members of this body have followed flickering lights in these dark and confusing times. Pardon and overrule what has been done unworthily, left undone, or done amiss.

And in thy great mercy, grant us peace—peace in our own hearts, peace in this dear land, and peace in all the earth, now and evermore. *Amen.*

❧ 9 ❧

O THOU Master of all good workmen, we come this day to honor one through whose deeds and lips in an anguished day thou didst speak—a universal man warmed with all laughter, tempered with all tears, whose sad and care-lined face mirrored the fearful struggle he led for the preservation of the Union as one and indivisible.

On this anniversary of his lowly birth we desire that—

> Our children shall behold his fame.
> The kindly, earnest, brave, foreseeing man
> Sagacious, patient, dreading praise, not blame.

In these days that test and try men's souls anew we would turn to thee with the dauntless faith which thy servant Abraham Lincoln proclaimed his own, as he said, "I recognize the sublime truth announced in the Holy Scripture and proved by all history that those nations are blessed whose God is the Lord. I believe that the will of God prevails. Without Him all human reliance is vain. Without the assistance of that Divine Being I cannot succeed—with that assistance I cannot fail."

We come to thee, his God and ours, with the sound of a great amen in our hearts to that creed by which he lived and we live as we lift our prayer to thee.

In the Redeemer's name. *Amen.*

❧ 10 ❧

Thou who art from everlasting to everlasting and who changeth not, abide with us, even as earth's joys grow dim and its glories pass away.

With tender solicitude we lift up in our prayer this day a great servant of the State whose iron will, moral standards, and passion for the coronation of righteousness and decency in international affairs, during these critical years, have been a bulwark of our liberties and the voice of America, as our free land has faced, and faces, ruthless foes bent on her destruction.

With courage which shames our cowardly fears and a faith deep-rooted in a religion that is his very life, thy servant John Foster Dulles stands in the valley of the shadow, while the nation he serves with such devotion and the free world cemented in unity by his wisdom and inflexible exertions lift grateful petitions for the smitten warrior who is facing the unseen with a cheer. May he fear no evil, as thy rod and thy staff comfort and sustain him.

As we face the crisis of the coming days, let each of us pray—

> God be in my head,
>   And in my understanding;
> God be in my eyes,
>   And in my looking;
> God be in my mouth,
>   And in my speaking;
> God be in my heart,
>   And in my thinking;
> God be at my end,
>   And at my departing.

In the dear Redeemer's name. *Amen.*

❧ 11 ❧

FATHER of all men, as our yearning spirits turn toward thee, help us to know that our coming is but futile mockery unless that coming draws us closer to one another and nearer to thy human family—our brothers and sisters—whoever and wherever they may be.

As we open our shuttered lives to thee, thy boundless love so freely given without measure and limit shames us with the sobering realization that no one of us has a right to live a self-centered life or confine our concern to some small, chosen group when the tides of human need, so wide and poignant, break moaning at our feet.

In thy clear light, as in a flaming vision, we see that nothing matters in the end except how any wisdom and strength with which we are entrusted is shared with those whose arms are stretched out to us in voiceless appeal.

Solemnize us with the certainty of judgment that awaits the response to that summons, whether it be poets singing deathless songs, artists giving form and color to beauty, seekers for knowledge driving shafts into new mines of truth, or statesmen with Christlike pity and sympathy directing the destinies of nations.

Above all else, save us from the supreme folly in a crucified world, in today's human agony, of holding ourselves safe and aloof.

We ask it in the dear Redeemer's name. *Amen.*

⚜ 12 ⚜

O THOU God of all men, blind and deaf would we be if we should bow in this chamber without a sense of solemn gladness that so much has been given to us. We come in the remembrance of lives greatly lived, whose record is our heritage. Be with us in deepened gratitude as we think of those who strove for truth and, when they found it, spoke it; those who could not see evil without crying out against it; those who felt in their own hearts the pain of the injustice done to others; and those who condemned oppression and fought for liberty.

Join us, we pray, in spirit to those who, with all their might, fought the good fight until they triumphed, raising the level of our common life and broadening the scope of human possibility.

In the midst of today's continuing struggle between the true and the false, between love and hate, grant us, by thy grace, new fortitude and reinforcement for the times in which we live, until by patience, persistence, and enduring courage we become sufficient for the tasks committed to our hands.

We ask it in the Redeemer's name. *Amen.*

❧ 13 ❧

OUR FATHER, enable, we pray, with the light of thy wisdom and the strength of thy might, those who in these fear-haunted times are here entrusted with the stewardship of the nation's life.

In our debates we face the things that divide this troubled world and set people against people, as their selfish interests clash. In prayer that is true and searching, we face thee and ourselves, in thy light.

Help us to see that the pride of nations, their greed, their lust for power, their aggressiveness against the rights of others, their deceitfulness and hypocrisy, are the very evils that corrode our own souls. And so we pray for ourselves, create in us clean hearts, O God.

> Breathe on [us], Breath of God,
> Fill [us] with life anew,
> That [we] may love what thou dost love,
> And do what thou wouldst do.

Amen.

❧ 14 ❧

OUR FATHER, for this hallowed moment hushing our words to silence, in sincerity and truth we bow before thee, who knowest the secrets of our hearts.

As at noontide we pause in reverence at this wayside altar the Founding Fathers set up, we look to thee. This is not just a passing gesture of devotion before going on our busy way with lives empty of thee. Rather, we come to ask thy guidance as thy servants here this day in the performance of their national stewardship face the demands of decision, the strain of toil, and the call of duty.

As together we go forward into this new decade of destiny, we pray that thy Spirit may heal the divisions that shorten the arm of our national strength in this great hour of history.

May we keep step not with the applause of men but with the drumbeat of thy purpose as we march in the ranks of those who do justly, love mercy, and walk humbly with their God.

In the dear Redeemer's name we pray. *Amen.*

❧ 15 ❧

O GOD, who art the resurrection and the life, as nature's tomb is flung open, we are thankful for the awakening beauty of a renewed earth. Give us the grace of receptivity, lest we walk in a garden of loveliness with eyes that do not thrill and hearts that do not sing.

As thy miracle of life is wrought anew in the tiniest bloom, in every green blade of grass, and in budding branches high against the bending sky, may the sheer wonder of it rebuke our chilling cynicism, the joy of it restore our faded hope, and its loveliness enrich our understanding of thy promise, which is sure.

In a spiritual springtime, may the high and the holy lay their touch upon us, and may our brief span of mortality be lighted with immortal dreams.

With the beauty of the Lord, our God, upon us, may we go forward with fortitude, honoring in the present all that is precious from the past, and keeping bright the promise of the future.

In the dear Redeemer's name, we ask it. *Amen.*

❧ 16 ❧

Our Father, from the beauty of the lilies, in the afterglow of earth's gladdest day, we come girdling ourselves with its deathless message as in the sense of the Eternal we take up our daily tasks again.

Amid all the fret and fever of present demands, may we be steadied by the conquering assurance that even when truth seems crushed to earth, with absolute certainty the third day comes, and banished truth is not vanquished truth; that error on the throne is always on the way to the dungeon, and right in the dungeon is always on the way to the throne.

With that invincible defense, strengthen us to face whatever the future holds, even though it be a cross, calm and confident that—

> There lives the beauty that man cannot kill;
> Yea, that shall kill all ugliness at last,
> And Christ risen, in love's white vesture,
> Moveth still among us.
> May we hold that creed and hold it fast!

We ask it in the name of the Redeemer, who saves us by the power of an endless life. *Amen.*

❧ 17 ❧

Our Father, maker of all things, judge of all men, hallowed be thy name.

In these epic days we would be the servants of thy will.

With the gaze of the nation and of the world fixed upon this chamber of governance, first of all we would write at the top of the record, "In the beginning God."

We would solemnly reaffirm the reverent declaration of those who long ago with radiant hope stepped upon the shores of this new land, "In the name of God, Amen."

We thank thee for the things that unite us—the passion for freedom, the hatred of tyranny whose aim is to erase thine image on each individual soul, the steadfast belief that in thy providence a purged America has come to the kingdom for such a time as this, the splendid vision of a redeemed earth when gnawing hunger, blighting superstition, and needless pain and misery will be but haunting memories. We thank thee for the things that unite us.

We thank thee for the things that divide us—for the un-fettered clash of mind on mind, for the right even to be wrong, for the summons to mobilize our own convictions to meet in intellectual and moral combat ideas that war against our own, none daring to molest or make us afraid. We are grateful for the things that divide us, for they are the hallmarks of men who are not cowed into coerced conformity.

For the triumph of the global crusade now raging, whose victory will mean that men everywhere will live in freedom, we set up our banners; and in this, thy glorious day, we lift our living nation a single sword to thee.

We ask it in the name of the Christ whose truth is marching on. *Amen.*

❦ 18 ❧

O GOD, so far above us, center and soul of every sphere, yet who dwellest in us: In the face of the One in whom thy fullest glory is revealed, thou hast told us that we are not to look for thee out on the rim of the universe—although the spangled heavens and the fruitful earth show thy handiwork—but that the deepest knowledge of thee is hidden in our own hearts and in the hearts of comrades who walk this earthly pilgrimage with us.

> Every virtue we possess,
> And every victory won,
> And every thought of holiness
> Are thine alone.

Wherever truth is spoken, thou dost speak. Wherever deeds are brave and selfless, thou art revealed.

In the unfolding pages of life's ripening experiences, we have learned that living by the best we know is the path to more certain knowledge; that in spiritual apprehensions it is the pure who are sure and who sense and see thee everywhere.

Help us to break away from the pull of small concerns which tie us to the ground and to be done with lesser things, as, yielding to thy will, our lives are put in orbit around the mastering purpose of thy redeeming love.

In the Redeemer's name. *Amen.*

≪ 19 ≫

OUR FATHERS' GOD, bowing at this wayside shrine which our fathers reared, we bring to thee the stress and strain of these testing times, praying that our jaded souls may find in thy presence the peace of green pastures and the still waters of the spirit.

We acknowledge that the wise provision of those who knelt about the cradle of our liberty, regarding the separation of church and state, did not decree the separation of religion and the state, knowing that spiritual verities are the very breath of the Republic.

In all the tangles of living together in the maze of human relationships through which, in legislative halls, those here chosen by the people grope their way, teach us anew by this moment of devotion that at its heart every great issue of life is spiritual.

Grant to thy servants in the ministry of public affairs the will to match vast needs with mighty deeds.

We ask it in the Redeemer's name. *Amen.*

❧ 20 ☙

O GOD our Father, who art love and light and truth, we turn unfilled to thee. In a world where the very foundations seem to be shaken, we cherish this hushed and hallowed moment which so long ago the Founding Fathers set apart as an altar of prayer at the day's beginning.

Here, with contrite hearts, we would be sure of thee and of spiritual resources before facing the high solemnities of waiting tasks. Grant that those who in this fateful day by the people's choice have been called to high places of state, facing responsibilities as heavy as the servants of the commonwealth have ever borne, may be filled with the spirit of wisdom and understanding, the spirit of knowledge, and the fear of thee.

In an hour when such vast issues are at stake for all the world, may those who here serve, conscious of the great tradition in which they stand, rise to greatness of vision and soul, as the anxious eyes of all the nations are fixed upon this chamber.

Send us forth, with full purpose of heart, in thy might unafraid, to meet the issues of this crucial year as in the name of the Lord, our God, we set up our banners.

We ask it in the dear Redeemer's name. *Amen.*

⚜ 21 ⚜

Our Father, trusting only in thy mercy, bringing nothing in our hands—our selfish hands, which we confess too often yield to the temptation to grasp at fleeting baubles—we wait in contrition for thy benediction at this shrine of thy forgiving grace.

We would face whatever the day may bring in the confidence of thy guidance, in the gladness of thy service, and in the solemn realization that there are no frontiers in the realm of neighborliness.

May the great causes that will mold the future of human destiny on this planet into the pattern of thy desire and design, that will heal the hurts of this sorely wounded world, that will create goodwill and usher in a just and abiding peace, challenge the best that is in us and gain the supreme allegiance of our love and labor as we serve our brief day in these fields of time.

We ask it in the name of the Master of all good workmen. *Amen.*

⚜ 22 ⚜

Almighty and everlasting God, as we bow in this quiet moment, dedicated to the unseen and eternal, confirm, we beseech thee, our abiding faith in the deep and holy foundations that the fathers laid, lest in foolish futility we attempt to build on sand instead of rock.

30

Make us alive and alert, we beseech thee, to the spiritual values that underlie the bitter struggle of these epic days.

In all our frantic seeking for satisfactions and solutions, if we find all except thee, we have nothing except vanity and our spirits remain still famished and thirsty.

To these, thy servants, who in the ministry of public service have been called by their counsel to help lead the peoples of the earth in these perplexing days, give a right judgment in all things. Grant them the sustaining grace both to will and to do the things that are good and acceptable in thy sight.

In the Redeemer's name we ask it. *Amen.*

❧ 23 ❧

OUR FATHER, who hast taught us that only in the reach of our love is the richness of our life, may no concern for self or ill will for others blur the goal of our glorious destiny among nations as the instrument of thy providence to free the earth from tyranny.

To this end, our God, bless America.

Thou seest, in spite of the worst things in us which we despise, that in our highest hours our deepest desire is to be the true servants of thy purpose in these times of social upheaval.

Grant us the grace, O Lord, to cherish and preserve evermore the heritage that is ours through the valor and virtue of those whose record, within these very halls, has helped make the greatness of our nation.

Inspire us so to follow their shining example that we may not only hold our inheritance as a sacred and precious trust, but, by our love and labor, leave it with increased luster to those who will come after us.

We ask it through riches of grace in Christ Jesus, our Lord. *Amen.*

🌿 24 🌿

Our Father, who dost overarch our fleeting years with thine eternity and undergird our weakness with thy strength: In the midst of the pressures of another week, as thy servants here face its vast concerns, with bowed heads and hearts we pause at this shrine of our spirits.

Without thee, even our wistful hopes for humanity are like withered leaves—once verdant and bright, but now brown and crumbled ruins blown upon a bitter wind.

Join us, we pray thee, in kinship to those who, in other times that tried men's souls, went on believing in beauty and love and God, in the midst of ugliness, hatred, and horror.

As we turn now to thee with deep craving for reality, we remember that we date this day's deliberations from the lowly cradle of One who died on the gallows of his day—mocked, reviled, insulted, outraged. Yet that torturing cross of defeat sways the future.

By its crimson sign which towers over the wrecks of time, may we conquer—in the dear Redeemer's name. *Amen.*

🌿 25 🌿

Our Father, in the heat and burden of days that drain our strength and demand our best, we would find the springs by the wayside—the living water whose elixir alone can refresh and restore our bodies and spirits, saving us from physical exhaustion, from spiritual impoverishment, from the numbness of routine, and from all cynicism and bitterness of heart. Through the sincere expression of differing appraisals in this chamber, may the final wisdom that charts the nation's course in these perilous days be higher than our own.

> Set our feet on lofty places;
>   Gird our lives that they may be
> Armored with all Christlike graces
>   In the fight to set men free.
> Grant us wisdom, grant us courage,
>   That we fail not man nor thee.

Amen.

❧ 26 ❧

OUR FATHER, we turn to thee for refuge from the noise and hurry of the world without, and from the tyranny of selfish moods and motives within.

May we fear only to be disloyal to the best we know, to betray those who love and trust us, and to disappoint thy expectations concerning us.

In a divided world where we see the dreadful penalties of gulfs of separation between humans who ought to stand together for mutual advantage, dedicate us in this anguished generation as builders of bridges across all the yawning spaces that mar this sadly sundered earth.

Help us this new day to meet its satisfactions with gratitude, its difficulties with fortitude, its duties with fidelity. Deliver us from petty irritations, which spoil the music of life and distort our perspectives. Bring us to the ending of the day unashamed and with a quiet mind because it is stayed on thee.

In the dear Redeemer's name we ask it. *Amen.*

≥ 27 ≤

O THOU God of life and light, our glad hearts thrill at the risen glory of the awakening earth robed in the blooming garb of spring.

Common bushes, lately so bare, are now aflame, and the time for the singing of birds has come. May a spiritual springtime make our own hearts like the garden of the Lord, where barren branches may be clothed with the beauty of holiness and flowers of humility and charity lift their fair petals above the fallow ground.

Prepare our hearts for the solemn glory of a malefactor's cross and for the splendor of an empty tomb. By the sign of that cross, on which thy Son gave his deathless spirit to thy keeping, strengthen us with might for the good fight we must wage against the gates of hell, knowing that joy is the fruit of sorrow; that strength comes out of weakness, and triumph out of failure; that song comes through sacrifice, gain through loss, and life through death.

In that faith may we fare forth, greeting the unknown with a cheer, sure that the third day cometh.

In Christ's conquering name we pray. *Amen.*

≥ 28 ≤

ETERNAL GOD, for this hallowed moment we would hush our feverish clamor to silence so that the voice of thy guidance may be heard as we face perplexing problems which tie us so closely to the seething world.

We are conscious that it is a world where tyrants still deal in fetters and chains as they attempt to shackle the free spirits of men made in thy image. We praise thee for the multitude in every land with whom we are joined, who cherish freedom of body and mind more than life itself.

Our Father, never let us forget that the treasure of freedom which we guard is in earthen vessels.

Save us, O Lord, from the hypocrisy of beholding a speck in another's eye without being aware of the log that is in our own eye.

Grant us inner discernment so that behind all the facades of security, privilege, and success we may honestly recognize the imperfect condition of our own lives, even as thou dost know it.

In all our striving to defend the truth, preserve in us the grace of self-criticism so that the living faith of the dead may not become the dead faith of the living.

We ask it in the name of the Redeemer who is the truth and the light. *Amen.*

1723185

✣ 29 ✣

ETERNAL FATHER, in a world that lieth in darkness swept by fitful winds of despair and doubt, for this hallowed moment we pause at this sheltered sanctuary of thy grace to make sure that the light within us is not dimmed. In this desperate hour of the nation's life, when the world's hope of a bright tomorrow is so largely committed to our frail hands, join us, we pray thee, to the great company of unconquered spirits who, in other evil times, have stood their ground, preserving the heritage of man's best, and whose flaming faith has made them like lighted windows amid the encircling gloom.

In this difficult and dangerous era, be thou our pillar of cloud by day, and of fire by night, as patiently and obediently we follow the kindly light of thy guidance. As deadly perils threaten the birthright of our liberties, help us to close our national ranks in a new unity. Hasten the coming of the radiant kingdom when each man's rule will be all men's good, and universal peace will lie like a shaft of light across the lands, and like a lane of beams across the sea.

We ask it in the Redeemer's name. *Amen.*

❦ 30 ❧

OUR FATHER, whose service is perfect freedom, we praise thee for the vision of liberty which, like a bow of promise, arches the dark skies and inspires mankind to overthrow all despotism and to break the fetters of oppression.

We praise thee, O Lord, for the judgment and wisdom of all those who, guided by thee, designed and founded the nations and institutions in which liberty is enshrined.

In this day of global conflict for the bodies and minds of man, we pray that thou wilt purge and cleanse our own hearts so that we may be found worthy to march with the armies of emancipation that bring release from the want and woe that beset so many millions of thy children and grind them into the dust of poverty.

In this day of battle when there is sounding forth a trumpet that must never know retreat, we praise thee for the courage, the labor, and the sacrifice of all those who are anywhere challenging and fighting the enemies of freedom.

Good Lord, deliver us from discouragement, appeasement of evil, indifference, petty prejudice, and all attitudes and actions and words that may hinder the achievement of a just and lasting worldwide peace.

We ask it in the name of Jesus Christ, our Lord. *Amen.*

❧ 31 ❧

GOD OF ALL mercies, as the pressing demands of another week summon thy servants here to high endeavor, we would pause for the sound of the trumpets in the morning—trumpets of faith and of hope.

In this national forum, with all its divergent human interests, we would rear an altar where a constant sense of eternal values may save us from spiritual decay, from moral cowardice, and from any betrayal of the highest public good. Only when our outlook is cleansed and corrected by constant communion with thee, and by the far horizons of the heavenly vision, can we see the transient in the light of the everlasting.

And so, like tillers of the soil who stand reverently with bowed heads, listening to the music of holy bells, we too would be strengthened with might in the inner man as each new day our ears wait for the sweet chimes of thy approval. Send us forth to meet an agitated world with a tranquillity that is strength and an inner integrity that is the courage of the soul.

In the dear Redeemer's name we ask it. *Amen.*

❧ 32 ❧

O LORD, our God, reverently we bow in the plenitude of thy mercies, which are new every morning.

We give thee thanks for the tasks that thou hast given us to accomplish and for the strength to do whatever is committed to our hands.

Help us to see that the lessons that thou hast set us to learn in thy great school of discipline are the steps to deeper comprehensions and to broader fields of service.

Amid all masquerades of error and the sophistries of the cynical which seek to deceive our day, lead us in the paths of righteousness and truth.

In this hour we would lift our prayer for the undergirding of thy sustaining grace for a trusted and beloved colleague of all in this chamber, upon whom have fallen the shadows of a deep personal grief.

Thou knowest the anxiety and concern of this servant of the nation who, while carrying the heavy responsibilities of his national stewardship, tenderly ministered to his dear companion of the long years as her strength ebbed away with the passing months.

And now may the honored president pro tempore of this body, whose patience and quiet poise are a source of strength to all his counselors here, himself be sustained by the consolations of thy grace and by a strength not his own, bringing the realization in his poignant loss that underneath are the everlasting arms.

We ask it in the name of that One who is the resurrection and the life. *Amen.*

⚜ 33 ⚜

OUR FATHER, thou hast set us in a world of wonder and beauty. Every new day we turn to thee, seeking deliverance from low motivation which would crucify wonder and beauty on a cross of personal greed or gain.

Help us to see and to feel that our highest joy in these fleeting days of mortal life is found in the loveliness of nature, in the lure of friendship, in the conquest of difficulty, and in the compensations of selfless service. In the preoccupation of this world capital, with vast issues that in their implications belt the earth, forgive us for our tendency to see too readily human failings in those close to us, and for our slowness in being aware of the virtues of those who toil by our side.

In this day of destiny, when in the fires of revolution all humanity seems molten, ready to be poured into new channels, may we be carried up into thy great purposes for thy human family. And may we find in thee, Father of mankind, above our human contentions, the goal of all our striving and the end of all our desiring, as we pray, "Thy kingdom come, thy will be done."

We ask it in the name of the Holy One who taught us thus to pray. *Amen.*

❧ 34 ❧

GOD OF ALL grace, thou hast taught us that in quietness and in confidence shall be our strength. On this day of world prayer, when around the earth the incense of intercession arises from the agonized needs of thy children, we, too, in this chamber of governance, would climb the world's great altar stairs which slope through darkness up to thee, the giver of all good.

We lift up our prayer for thy endowment of spiritual might upon the godly women of all the churches in this our capital city, who are reverently bowing this very hour at an altar set up in this white-domed shrine of each patriot's devotion, asking for thy healing grace as the only balm in Gilead for the ills of this sundered and wounded world.

On this appointed day we would join the hosts under all skies in the mystery of united prayer by which more things are wrought than this world dreams of. We do not ask for thy bestowal upon us of any material thing. We ask only that thou wouldst make us men and women of pure hearts, purged from the mire of moral failure, free from the lure of selfish advantage and of the prejudice that blinds our inner eyes and warps our judgment.

So above all, in turmoils without and within, day by day we would find—

> A little place of mystic grace
> Of self and sin swept bare
> Where [we] may look into Thy face
> And talk with Thee in prayer.

In the dear Redeemer's name we ask it. *Amen.*

❧ 35 ❧

GOD OF the living and of the living dead, as in this hour we bow in the shadow of a people's grief, thou dost hear the sobbing of a stricken nation. But we come with the comfort that thou knowest what is in the darkness, and that the darkness and the light are both alike to thee.

For the stewardship in the brief but epochal years of the young and gallant captain who has fallen at his post, we give thanks to thee, the Master of all good workmen. In the profile of courage, of vision, and of faith that John F. Kennedy etched upon the darkened sky of these agitated times, in his exalted place of leadership, we behold the image of our America, which alone will make sure the survival of our freedom.

Now that the valorous sword has fallen from his lifeless hands, he seems to be calling to us in the unfinished tasks that remain.

> Others will sing the song
> Finish what I began
> What matters I or they

Mine or another's day
So the right word be said
And life the purer made.

In the nation's poignant loss, may there come to those whose hands are at the helm of this dear land of our faith and love the vision that fortified thy prophet of old as he bore witness: "In the year that King Uzziah died I saw the Lord sitting upon a throne, high and lifted up. . . ."

In this year of a tragic death, may there be granted to us a vision of the preeminent spiritual verities that abide and undergird and outlast the life and death of any mortal servant of great causes who toils for a while in these fields of time in the sense of the Eternal, and then falls on sleep.

We pray in the name of the risen Christ who hath brought life and immortality to light. *Amen.*

❧ 36 ❧

FATHER of men and nations, thou knowest that on these black-bordered days our heavy hearts have been saying, "Earth's joys grow dim, its glories pass away."

But we turn to thee, who art from everlasting to everlasting. We know that a riderless steed, upon which millions have gazed with appalled eyes, is not a symbol of a leaderless nation, and that history assures us that in every crisis thou dost raise up men to carry on thy mission for the redemption of humanity.

We are heartened to know that when any leader falls, thy truth goes marching on—always.

At this noontide which succeeds the day of mourning, when the nation stopped to weep and ponder, we turn to unfinished

Prayers 35 and 36 were given Monday, November 25, 1963, and Tuesday, November 26, respectively, after the death of President John F. Kennedy.

tasks with a new assurance of the invincibility of righteousness
and truth. Like a rainbow arching the darkened sky will be the
remembrance that to America in her shocked grief, there hastened the highest spokesmen of the world's nations, speeding
around the earth to stand together in a temple of divine worship, witnessing to an essential kinship with the eternal principles to which this Republic, under any leader, is dedicating her
might.

And now as these heralds of goodwill return to their own
capitals so far away, we would lift to thee, with hearts strangely moved, Kipling's prayer:

> The tumult and the shouting dies;
> The captains and the kings depart;
> Still stands thine ancient sacrifice,
> An humble and a contrite heart;
> Lord God of hosts, be with us yet,
> Lest we forget, lest we forget.

Amen.

❧ 37 ❧

O THOU Master of all good workmen, with the
passing from this mortal stage of a dedicated servant of thine
and of the nation, Douglas MacArthur, we now praise famous
men—men renowned for their power, giving counsel by their
understanding, leaders of the people, wise and eloquent in their
instruction.

Such leave a name behind them so that their praises might
be reported. We give thanks that thine eternal principles of
righteousness, which the contaminating evils of the world cannot tarnish or erode, are so often made flesh in human personalities.

42

Especially this day we thank thee, our God, and take courage from the uncorrupted and uncompromising record of this great captain of our time, in whose undaunted faith through all the years of his pilgrimage there ever sang—

> Then conquer we must,
> When our cause it is just,
> And this be our motto,
> "In God is our trust."

Now that he has gone from our physical sight and side, may he return to our troubled times in a renewed determination of the Republic to face any foe and to pay any price, not in order that America may conquer, but that the starry ideals that give luster to freedom's banners may come to their coronation under all skies. For the fulfillment of all our fallen hero's dreams, as his brave soul goes marching on, we commend his conquering spirit into thy hands.

We ask it in the dear Redeemer's name. *Amen.*

🌿 38 🌿

O GOD from whom all blessings flow, as we stretch lame hands of prayer to thee, grant us the benediction of thy healing peace. Draw very near to us. Teach us to weave the concerns of these troubled days into the perspective of long years.

The cries of the crowds about us only bring us to confusion without and perplexity within. As the words of this chamber are hushed to silence in this solemn, searching moment, breathe upon our thinking with thy truth, breathe upon our understanding with thy light, breathe upon our attitudes with thy love.

May the heavy pressures of the world not mold us, but may we be so strengthened with might in the inner man that we may help mold the world nearer to the fashion of thy righteous will. At this common altar of prayer may we find a unit that ties us together, even amid all the diversities of our thought and the perplexing problems whose attempted solutions so often tend to divide us in our judgment.

Beset by the confusion of these days, when honest and sincere men differ, may we never forfeit our own self-respect or the confidence of those who trust us, as we dedicate our highest and best to the service of the nation.

In the dear Redeemer's name we ask it. *Amen.*

⚜ 39 ⚜

OUR FATHER, from the jubilation of the nation's joyous remembrance of heroic bequests from the costly past, we come with bowed heads and grateful hearts, praying that grace may be ours to hallow the deeds of yesterday and to remember that eternal vigilance, not annual observances, is the price of liberty, and that each generation must earn the right to keep it.

In all the national agitation that privileges guaranteed to all shall be open to all, may there be among all elements of our favored people a solemn acknowledgment of the rights which the nation, whose very breath is freedom, requires for itself of every loyal citizen.

Give, we pray, to those who are anxiously claiming their birthright the realization that among the rights claimed by the Republic is the obligation of those who enjoy liberty to practice the Golden Rule in all human relationships, to give loyal obedience to the nation's laws, to strive to increase the store of understanding and goodwill, so that each citizen worthy of freedom, jealous of the total strength of the commonwealth, shall have as his highest joy not what he takes but what he gives. *Amen.*

⅙ 40 ⅞

GOD OF ALL grace and mercy, from the strife and confusion of the speech of men, we seek to enter the sanctuary of prayer, where an altar has been set up by those who launched our Republic.

We pray for height in our lives. We need altitude. Above the divisive goals of these baffling days, lift us to some high outlook where we may catch inspiring vistas.

We pray for breadth in our lives. Save us from being shut in by the narrowness of our interests, and even by the vindictiveness of our irritations. Lift us high so that we may see broadly, with more understanding care, the whole vast circle of human yearning to escape from misery.

We pray for length of outlook and of vision. The immediacies of the present days, with their stark poignancy, stare at us. But, O God, in whose sight a thousand years are like yesterday, give us a long look, because we lift our gaze from the dusty valley of daily toil to the hills of help which stab the far horizon.

And so, with powers that are lifted and broadened and lengthened, may our individual lives be more fit to be the channels of thy redeeming purposes for all mankind. *Amen.*

SPIRES OF
THE SPIRIT

Cathedral
Bells

"BLESS THESE BELLS," intoned the dean of the Washington Cathedral. "Bless these bells," petitioned the Episcopal bishop of the diocese. In the hearts of a reverent multitude, gathered in awed silence in the lingering twilight of the September Sunday, there was the sound of a great Amen.

The dedication of these bells, as a potent witness to Christian faith, was an event of national—even worldwide—significance. Their dulcet melody and clanging certainty is ringing out in what is being acclaimed as the most inspiring chiming choir on the continent. Each of the fifty-three bells of the carillon, from the largest—the Bourdon bell weighing twelve tons—to the smallest—tipping the scales at only fifteen pounds—flings out the glad proclamation "I believe." These bells voice America's answer to today's blasphemous denials of the Father who holds the whole world in his hands.

The priority of these bells in any expert appraisal of musical excellence is suggested by the enthusiastic comment of an outstanding music critic who usually ladles out praise by the "thimbleful." He said, "These bells of the cathedral carillon have a sweetness and power, a majestic beauty, and a brilliant sonority I've never heard in any of a dozen of the world's other carillons."

To think of this occasion in the nation's capital as a matter of special interest to only one city would be like announcing an eclipse of the sun under "local events," as a certain newspaper once did. These bells, now safely lifted to their lofty home atop the exquisite pinnacled central tower of the Cathedral of Saint Peter and Saint Paul, are a dream come true. They have overtones of deep import in a fear-haunted world where, as never before, spiritual verities are pitted against rampant principalities and powers of entrenched evil.

There have been stirring scenes galore in the beautiful city on the Potomac. Spectacular pageants have mirrored historic celebrations. Present at the dedication of the cathedral bells were those whose national city memories run back half a century and who, with hearts strangely warmed, declared that the scene in and around the Gothic glory of the growing cathedral was unmatched in its moving significance. For the thousands gathered in the gloaming of that perfect September day, it was a climactic hour that ranked high among events staged in the capital during all the years stretching back to the first president of the infant Republic, who expressed the hope that some day there should be a great cathedral in the capital of the nation that calls him "Father."

On this never-to-be-forgotten evening, rising majestically above the massed throng were the soaring arches of the noble edifice crowned now by the lacy loveliness of the Gloria in Excelsis Tower, of which every spiritually sensitive American with an inward sense of the eternal can be justly proud.

Now, after more than half a century of building, the central tower, through the skilled labor of many months, has climbed to its destined place in the skyline to a height exceeding that of the famed Washington Monument. Its visibility from various approaches to the capital make it regnant among all other structures, as does the message it proclaims. Thus, at the dedication a priceless gift was presented to all who have ears to hear, and hearts to feel. It was offered to those who, from near and far, will partake of a royal feast of heavenly melody freely offered, like June, to the poorest comer.

And so these bells become a wealthy asset to the spiritual riches of the city that belongs to every American and to the nation. They are bells ordained to sing and proclaim a wordless certainty which dispels moods of cynical disbelief. These bells speak ever of unity. They know nothing of border, or breed, or birth. A belfry may belong to one church—but not the bells! Their aerial symphony steals into rooms even when the doors are shut. Their resounding tones remind all who really listen that religion is bigger than the measure of man's mind. They speak a language that casts aside all pettiness and bigotry as they utter glowing words about God and man, life and duty, lest men's hearts turn to water and their strength disappear.

These bells are the proud product of the renowned Taylor Bellfoundry in England, where, under that name, the fashioning of bells has been perfected for more than four hundred years. They wait to leap into action at the touch of the skilled carillonneur, whose pulpit is a lofty keyboard. They are the memorial gift of Bessie Juliet Kibbey, who, half a century ago, in the beginning days of the cathedral, set aside the funds for a carillon in memory of her grandparents.

Hawthorne once said:

A Gothic cathedral is surely the most wonderful work which mortal man has yet achieved, so vast, so intricate, and so profoundly simple, with such strange, delightful recesses in its grand figure, so difficult to comprehend within one idea and yet all so consonant that it ultimately draws the beholder and his universe into its harmony. It is the only thing in the world that is vast enough and rich enough.

As prophets of the evangel stand up to preach in the white pulpit so far below the lofty bell choir, may there be repeated the experience of a prophet of long ago, Elisha, who said, " 'Now bring me a minstrel.' And when the minstrel played, the power of the LORD came upon him."

The marvel of it all is that these cathedral bells are yours, whatever your name or sign.

> As if a choir
>   In robes of fire,
> Were singing here—
>   No shout nor rush,
> But hush
>   For God is here!

Beyond
Grief

IN the tinted glory of a mellow Washington autumn the most appealing symbol of the bittersweet mystery of life is in an ancient city of the dead, Rock Creek Cemetery. It is Augustus Saint-Gaudens' famed statue, which for some strange reason has had attached to it the title *Grief*. That popular appellation tells nothing with regard to its deep meaning.

Henry Adams, who in memory of his wife gave to a master workman the sacred task of conceiving and fashioning a sculptured sacrament which would please the eyes and search the souls of oncoming generations, often called the finished statue *The Peace of God*. A very distinguished statesman, in a letter to Adams, gave this appraisal: "The monument is indescribably noble and imposing. It is full of poetry, infinite wisdom, a past without beginning and a future without end, a repose after limitless experience, a peace to which nothing matters."

The greenish bronze figure of a seated woman within the incredible perfection of the folds of her ample cloak is the high altar of a secluded sylvan sanctuary, guarded by evergreens and holly trees, through whose draperies little truant waves of sunlight pass to dance upon the pebbled floor of this mystic chapel of the living dead. The figure is an Alpine peak in art. Competent critics with almost one accord acclaim the Rock Creek Adams Memorial as Saint-Gaudens' masterpiece, surpassing his *Christ* in the Phillips Brooks Memorial in Boston and his *Lincoln* in Chicago. Alexander Woollcott declared it "the most beautiful thing ever fashioned by the hand of man on this continent."

To live in the city that wears this creation as a wondrous gem and never to take the path worn by those drawn as by a magnet from half a world away to gaze upon this miracle of spiritual significance and artistic perfection, is like being in Paris and never seeing the *Venus de Milo* or *Mona Lisa,* or in Milan and missing *The Last Supper.*

When the world began to talk about this perfect flowering of Saint-Gaudens' genius, someone meeting him ventured upon a subject the artist always seemed reluctant to discuss. Asked the meaning of his Rock Creek creation, he replied slowly and with deep feeling: "Some call it the Peace of God, some Nirvana. It is the human soul face to face with the greatest of all mysteries." To demand an explanation seems like insisting that the meaning of Beethoven's Fifth Symphony, which Saint-Gaudens greatly loved, should be captured in a mathematical equation. In the highest realms ultimate meaning always breaks through formulas and escapes.

Saint-Gaudens' purpose, evidently, was not to answer final questions, but to raise them. The answer depends upon the one face to face with that tranquil countenance with the deep eyes that neither frown nor smile. To some, the effect of the mysterious figure is to induce a shuddering sense of negation and futility. To others, the brooding form represents the philosophic rather than the religious approach to what men call death. There is evidence that Adams desired the memorial to express the intellectual acceptance of the inevitable, whatever that might be.

This hooded woman was not meant as a modern sphinx. She does speak to those who have ears to hear. Yet she will not murmur her secrets to just anybody. To those who come to her with an undimmed faith she speaks assuringly from a realm where there is peace beyond these raucous voices. She is beyond self, beyond sense, beyond sham and show, beyond mortality, beyond strife and striving, beyond grief.

Here, with a multitude of white stones surrounding and a world city sweeping up to the very gates of the cemetery, sitting unheeding in this calm and sure retreat, is life—but it is life ten minutes after death.

No wonder John Galsworthy made one of his characters, a cultured Englishman who visited this memorial, remark with awe that it was "the best thing he had come across in America, the one that gave him the most pleasure, in spite of all the water he had seen at Niagara and those skyscrapers in New York." As he gazed, a falling crimson oak leaf lodged in his lapel, another on his knee. But so engrossed was he that he did not brush them off. For he was looking too intently at "the woman who had passed beyond grief, as she sat in a frozen acceptance deeper than death itself—very remarkable." The comment of the Britisher as he left was, "They ought to make America sit here once a week."

This raises the question: Have you ever sat there, on that judgment seat, letting that silent figure speak to the immortal part of you?

> O tranquil eyes that look so calmly down
> Upon a world of passion and of lies,
> O calm, unchanging eyes, that once have
>   shone
> With these our fitful fires, that burn and
>   cease
> With light of human passion, human tears,
> And know that after all the end is
>   PEACE.

A Date with
a Tree

On the shady grounds surrounding the Capitol are many noble trees. Most of them are tagged with their botanical designations. But tags do not explain the spell of a tree.

A glorious American elm proudly lifts its leafy, lofty branches and spreads its benign shade near the famous white dome, which, shining like alabaster in the darkness, is an inspiring symbol of America at its best. There are a number of other lordly trees standing sentinel near the nation's legislative halls, which remind us of the phrase of the poet Keats, who always was awed by tall oaks—"Those green-robed Senators of majestic woods!"

A nationally known legislator, breaking away for a while from the relentless grind of office, committee room, and forum, was seen walking across a grassy knoll to the sylvan spot where this majestic elm holds kingly sway, its verdant robes flowing with regal and sacred grace.

Said the senator to a colleague he chanced to meet, "I'm turning aside long enough to pay my respects to yonder magnificent elm." "You mean," said the other in evident approval, "you are about to call on a tree!" And why not? Trees have been the intimates and the inspiration of some of the tallest among the sons of men.

However, their confidence may be earned only by one who, in spite of crowded schedules, still finds time for a date with a tree.

Thoreau, the Hermit of Walden Pond, who, by example, undertook to show his generation how many energy- and time-devouring things men and women could get along without, once excused himself from a persistent visitor by explaining that he had to leave to keep an engagement with a tree. The biggest and busiest of men have never felt that they had to apologize for keeping a tryst with a tree.

Frequently the genial Autocrat of the Breakfast Table, Oliver Wendell Holmes, had a date with a certain grand old oak at Beverly, Massachusetts, which he never approached without a bow and genuflection. Of that tree he said to the friend upon whose land it stood, "Ah, John, you think you own that tree! But you don't. It owns you!"

James Russell Lowell, who once said he cared more for his trees than his books, advised that every man should sometimes retreat into the heart of the woods and closet himself in the rustling privacy of leaves, so that there he may find a peaceful pleasure.

Wordsworth suggested in deathless phrases what enrichment may come to the spirit as recompense for a date with trees, when he wrote:

> One impulse from a vernal wood
> May teach you more of man,
> Of moral evil and of good,
> Than all the sages can.

An outstanding essayist on whose rhythmic pages words are set to music, and who is remembered by those privileged to know him as a courtly, cultured, knightly personality, passionately loved trees. He believed that a tree comes nearer to having a soul than any other creation in the vegetable kingdom.

No wonder in the history of worship we find that groves were the first temples. And how trees have figured in the great Judeo-Christian tradition! Moses, whose colossal form seems to bestride those early centuries, had an engagement with a tree which, for him, proved a vital factor in his destiny and that of the horde of slaves he freed. He turned aside to see and listen as a bush burned and was not consumed. On that spot the awesome commission of the God of Abraham and Isaac and Jacob was put into his hands.

The psalmist likened a man who delights in the law of the Lord to a tree planted by the streams of water, which brings forth fruit in its season, and he declared that the righteous shall flourish like the palm tree and grow like a cedar in Lebanon.

With delicate pathos Sidney Lanier, in his "Ballad of Trees and the Master," whispered that "the olives they were not blind to him," that "the little gray leaves were kind to him" and "the thorn-tree had a mind to him" in the ordeal of the dark garden. Then, after that agony under the trees,

> Out of the woods my Master came,
> Content with death and shame.
> When Death and Shame would woo him last,
> From under the trees they drew him last:
> 'Twas on a tree they slew him—last
> When out of the woods he came.

The One Touch More

THE yellow- and pink-petaled banners of the early summer are but the advance guard of the flower parade to announce that the battalions of roses are on the way. But the first frail, ephemeral blossoms pass so soon; they seem just to wave at us and then are gone—perishing tinted things born for only a brief day. However, they signal gayly, "The roses are coming."

Then when June of the rare days approaches, treading softly in velvet slippers, the procession of roses bursts into view and gardens, porches, yards, fences, trellises, and arbors become reviewing stands where, with enraptured senses, the radiant regiments in their enchanting uniforms can be watched. They keep step into the shortening days, with the rear guard still marching bravely, with hardy tread, when trees are bare and frost is on the pumpkin.

Who doubts that, if a popularity contest could be registered at the swinging garden gate, the rose would emerge as the best-loved bloom? The rose award for entrancing witchery is based partly on the glory of the curved, silky petals, like floral gems, and the delicate fragrance, a heavenly incense. However, the decision goes to the rose not because of any ecstatic catalog of surpassing excellences but because of a subtle mystery—intangible, tantalizing, evasive. It is an indefinable something, a one-touch-more. It is the never-quite-solved riddle of the rose.

For some, the climax of this floral summer symphony is the red rose, which, to Oliver Wendell Holmes, always symbolized the gayety and vitality of youth.

For some, it is the white rose. A wealthy man with a famous garden grew only white roses because they had been the favorites of his wife, who had passed on. There was always a vase of them wistfully arranged near her portrait. The lonely and usually reticent husband confided to a visitor, "She passionately loved her white roses, and seldom went out without taking a handful of them to somebody."

For some, including the grateful writer of this rose rhapsody, a yellow rose embodies the quintessence of all floral loveliness. But red, or pink, or white, or yellow, there is that something which breaks through language and escapes.

We feel the spell of the mystery hidden in a rose as we bend to inhale the fragrance even in the garden of human graces and virtues. Was not the Perfect Life—Christ—called the Rose? Said one whose profession led him to mingle with folk of every shade of humanity, "I know people whose hearts are perfect gardens of roses. You cannot spend ten minutes in their company without detecting the delicate and delicious aroma. Their hearts are full of roses." But both fragrant roses and fragrant virtues require care, discipline, and sacrifice.

In a fascinating book about roses as they are so lovingly cultivated in England, the author tells about the superb blossoms he found to his surprise at a poor workingmen's show. His expectations were not very high, for it was out of season and in a poverty-stricken district. He visited the humble cottages and inquired how such wonderful roses were produced. It was the same story everywhere—sacrifice, self-denial! One workman, before it was light in the morning, trudged two miles to tend his precious rosebushes before breakfast and then rushed off to the factory. Another tumbled out, in a bitter, frosty night, and stripped the blankets from his own bed to wrap around his favorite bushes. For them and theirs the bright roses added some mystical thing to the drab ugliness of the commonplace. In the midst of squalor, roses spoke of the second mile, beyond drudgery.

In one of his scintillating essays Emerson argues that fondness for floral decoration is a delicate and unconscious tribute that we pay to the Infinite, the Invisible, the Yonder. It is a mystic touch beyond the treadmill of the required.

Following a Sunday evening service in a hospital in New York, a visiting minister was taken through the wards by a doctor so that he might say a word of hope to the sufferers. By the side of each bed the preacher noticed a little vase containing a single rose. The surgeon explained that this symbol of cheer always awaited each patient when he or she arrived. "Of course," he added, "later there will be bouquets galore from friends. But this is what we call the one touch more." Later that night the preacher, who had seen the "Spires of the Spirit" rising above that single little flower vase, wrote these lines in the quiet of his study:

> Beside each bed a vase was set,
>   And in each vase a golden rose,
> Sweet sign that God and man had met
>   Where love divine most richly glows.
> O noble heart! O knightly soul!
>   Thine is the gift angels adore:
> Heal, thou, men's bodies, make them whole,
>   But add—like roses—one touch more.

Discoverers of America

ONCE more, in October's mellow days, the New World pauses to honor Columbus. In four lines Joaquin Miller caught, for the two hundred million who now live in the United States, the thrill of the epic adventure as the terrified crew turned to their leader with dread alarm and entreaties that he turn back:

> "Brave Admiral, say but one good word:
> What shall we do when hope is gone?"
> The words leapt like a leaping sword:
> "Sail on! sail on! sail on! and on!"

And so the discovery of America was not the accomplishment of only three tiny ships and the intrepid navigator whose name and fame are immortal. That discovery has been the unfinished task of many ships and many men. There have been many discoverers of America. More than a half-century ago Senator Elbert J. Beveridge was discovering America when he declared: "God's great purposes for America are revealed in a manner which surpasses the intentions of the Congress and cabinets. We cannot fly from our world duties. It is ours to execute the purposes of faith that have driven us to be greater than our small intentions."

Longfellow was discovering America when he sang, "Humanity, with all her fears, with all her hopes of future years, is hanging breathless on thy fate."

There are grateful people in many countries who, through the CARE crusade of sharing, are discovering the real America. She is being discovered as the Good Samaritan by various nations that are receiving food for the hungry, medicine for the sick, clothing for those who desperately need it, and knowledge for self-help, which is the key to more abundant life.

To those over whose penury and misery she bends with compassion, America is indeed discovered as a land of hope and glory. Weakness a half-world away is leaning on her strength. Jaded peoples are drinking at her fountains. Fearful, threatened people are trusting in her might. People who sit in darkness are seeing her great light. And, thank God, America has been discovered not only by the friends who need her undergirding but also by her enemies. Every sinister power on earth has discovered America. How could they help it? There she stands, with colossal power, moral and material, blocking the way to world dominion by so-called people's democracies, which is but a false face for the hideous countenance of total slavery.

William Tyler Page was discovering America in the creed he fashioned, which is a summary of the fundamental principles of American political faith as set forth in its greatest documents, its worthiest traditions, and its greatest leaders. In the words of the Page creed:

I believe in the United States of America as a Government of the people, by the people, for the people; whose just powers are derived from the consent of the governed; a democracy in a republic, a sovereign Nation of many sovereign States; a perfect Union one and inseparable; established upon those principles of freedom, equality, justice and humanity for which American patriots sacrificed their lives and fortunes. . . .

In that great statement an outstanding American was discovering anew our America!

The discovery of America in its significance as a political, intellectual, and moral force in the world was not the business of Columbus only. It is the business of all of us to discover for our own time the full meaning and significance of America for itself and all the world.

Angela Morgan, shortly before she died, discovered America for us all in these inspiring lines:

> To the crippled and weak of the
>   nations
> Hast thou uttered the Master's
>   decree,
> And thy work, it hath set the
>   foundations
> Of that glorious kingdom to be.
> Come swiftly, O wondrous
>   tomorrow
> That shall render to justice a
>   soul,
> When the nations shall rise from
>   their sorrow,
> The sick and the helpless be
>   whole.
> Let us cry it aloud from the
>   steeple,
> Let us shout where the darkness
>   is hurled,
> Lo, look to the light of all people—
> America, Torch of the World!

One Good Scoop of
Flattery

OUR bodies are harps with a thousand strings. The hands of skillful manipulators sometimes can so soothe and adjust a physical organism which is out of tune that harmony returns and the music of bodily well-being is restored. If healing hands can do that in the realm of the flesh, how much more do the spiritual chords of our being respond to the touch of understanding hands as they gently sweep over the vibrating scale! But how melody is changed to jarring discord when the playing hands are those of disregard and discouragement! It is love alone that sees the best glimmering through the worst. Like the Master of men, who was Incarnate Love, it believes in the possibilities and capabilities of the human heart in spite of the present stage, or even of lapses.

In the realm of the spirit, when some frail human's outlook is clouded with failure, fear, self-depreciation, and a sense of inadequacy, there is no treatment that is more of an elixir than what is commonly referred to as "a pat on the back." To be sure, that is borrowing a term of physical contact to describe a reaction of the mind. But that "pat" is often the push that changes fear to faith and failure to success, in a given venture.

A slap on the back may be nothing more than the exuberant gesture of a boisterous extrovert whose violent greeting seldom is the expression of deep friendship. But a quiet, unobtrusive pat on the back may change a darkened day into a vista of blue skies and singing birds. A pat on the back, if it is a sign of approval, belief, appreciation, and confidence, may be one of the most precious things you can give to a comrade struggling by your side.

It can be said that Jesus gave Simon Peter a pat on the back when he called him "rock," at the very time Peter was counted, by men who had experienced his fickleness, as the most fluctuating one of the group. That attitude, assuring him that the Master was confident he would make it, that he was on the way to deserve the name Jesus had given him, was a powerful reinforcement in the battle for sainthood he was waging.

Some time ago an elderly minister passed to his reward. One of the best-known contemporary preachers in the world today gratefully declared, at the time of this older man's passing, that he decided to enter the ministry because of a "pat on the back" that this man gave him, when he said some generous things about his first sermon, which was faltering and faulty. "Without that pat," the younger man said, "I would have turned aside from the ministry."

When Charles Dickens passed through a period of frustration as a factory hand, it was a friend, John Black, who strengthened his self-respect, who helped him keep his chin up. At the height of his fame as a novelist Dickens, with deep appreciation, wrote: "Dear old Black! My first hearty out-and-out appreciator!"

If parents would but watch for chances to praise their children honestly, instead of by constant criticism giving them a failure complex, such pats on the back would almost unbelievably strengthen the morale of the youngsters, too often measured by adult yardsticks. When a boy of ten conducted himself at a dinner table in such a way that his mother knew he had remembered her training, I heard her whisper a word of pride. His look of satisfaction was her reward.

What wives who take their husbands' toil and even their successes as a matter of course could do for their companions by occasional pats on the back! Once an English author published a book with a pointed and poignant dedication: "To my wife, whose lack of interest in this volume has been my constant despair." And how the wilted flowers in many a woman's life would revive like a garden after a refreshing shower if she should experience the "pat on the back" the book of Proverbs records regarding a good woman:

> Her children rise up and call her blessed;
> her husband also, and he praises her:
> "Many women have done excellently,
> but you surpass them all."

This, of course, is not a plea for unmeant flattery, which often is only shabby insincerity. But, as suggests a well-known religious leader, there are millions of people who would be uplifted and helped if they could have once in a while "one good scoop of flattery" from someone they trust. It is amazing what an occasional good scoop of flattery—not frothy "soft soap" but an honest appraisal of one's potentialities—will do to keep some discouraged person on his feet.

We suggest a new honorary degree for those who do most for humanity and who are largely responsible for other people's accomplishments: P.O.B.—Patters on the Back. The only difficulty is that there would not be colleges enough to confer the degree on those who deserve it.

> There are two kinds of people,
>   You meet them
> As you journey along on life's
>   track,
> The people who take your strength
>   from you,
> And the people who put it all back.

The Prophecy of
the Palms

IN every city and hamlet of America palm branches are being waved on this day of faith and prophecy. Around the world the Festival of the Palms holds sway. It does not matter what one's belief may be with regard to a dozen other debatable matters; in the Western world the credo of Palm Sunday finds almost universal acceptance. Even in the manacled and muzzled church of Russia the palms express a deathless faith the police state cannot kill.

A great hymn, the tune of which ironically comes out of Russia, declares:

> God the all righteous One!
> Man hath defied thee;
> Yet to eternity standeth thy word;
> Falsehood and wrong shall not
>   tarry beside thee.

That is the message of the palms under capitalism, socialism, or communism. It is the creed enshrined in the "Battle Hymn of the Republic" with the words "Glory, glory, hallelujah! His truth is marching on."

Every green branch in the hands of multitudes around the planet this day is a confident assertion that truth crushed to earth shall rise again.

And so the palms point to terrific realities of the universe which one can ignore only if he wants to live in a fool's paradise. The laws the palms declare cannot be broken without breaking the offender. The causes the palms symbolize are the inevitable causes.

The palms are uttering the great, creative words of human speech—truth, liberty, justice, goodness, beauty, and brotherhood. These are invincible and irresistible because they are the values at the heart of the universe. These things are the very life of God. Therefore, they are eternal and indestructible; they cannot be defeated.

Everything about the Lone Rider of Palm Sunday speaks of the hollowness of pomp, the pretense of pride, the ashes of ambition, the vanity of power, the disillusionment of fame, the deception of wealth. Pilate could appeal to a power that seemed final—the might of an authoritarian state. Jesus could appeal only to a power that to many people does not seem to be power at all—the power of the spirit, of meekness, and of love. And, what happened a few hours after the palms had been waved and the Hosannas shouted? Jesus was dead! Pilate had triumphed. That is what always happens when Pilate encounters Christ. From dawn to dark the sword always conquers the spirit. In any given twenty-four hours truth and right are no match for the heaviest battalions.

The clear eyes of the One whom the judge sentenced to death were on a distant goal as he gazed past both the palms and Pilate. That condemned prisoner had stood with his back against the moral pillars of the universe when he declared, "Heaven and earth will pass away, but my words will not pass away." He could appeal only to a power that to most people did not, and does not, seem to be power at all—the power of the spirit, the might of meekness. Yet the name of Pilate is rescued from oblivion solely because of that one day's association with the silent captive before him.

Long ago the world was through with Pilate. But the world is not through with Jesus; it is through without him! The principles of the Rider of Palm Sunday are woven into the moral pattern of the universe. His precepts are the very laws of life.

Under the mighty dome of the Invalides in Paris, I looked down at the impressive blood-red tomb of Napoleon, the little Corsican who waded through blood to a selfish throne. Looking up from the sarcophagus, I beheld the uplifted form of the world's Redeemer upon his cross, dazzling with splendor as the sunshine streamed through a nearby stained-glass window. I thought of the words of the lonely Napoleon on Saint Helena: "Charlemagne, Alexander and I built great empires; but they were founded on force and have crumbled away. But Jesus of Nazareth founded his kingdom on love, and there are millions today who would die for him."

A Glorious
Gamble

CHRIST'S entire public ministry was a daring bet. No wonder that his friends tried to pull him back; to do what he was bent on doing seemed to spell certain suicide. He was walking into a trap set by his enemies. Surely, to be a cautious and even compromising prophet was better than being a dead one! But his faith made a date with destiny inevitable. He knew that the nails must pierce either his faith or his flesh.

The pageantry of the ephemeral hosannas did not deceive Jesus. He was riding on to die. He had staked his life on the belief that truth is stronger than error, that love is stronger than hate, that meekness is mightier than pride, and that life at last will conquer death. For that faith, "He was a gambler, and took his life and threw it for a world redeemed."

Christ risked everything on the absolute conviction that even a cross could not stop him. As the grim gallows of that day loomed nearer and nearer, he declared with exultant confidence: "I am . . . the truth" and "I, when I am lifted up from the earth, will draw all men to myself."

And so Christianity is forever the parable of a fighting faith. There is really no faith worth talking about that is not worth fighting for. We will fight to the bitter end for anything that possesses our souls. Where and when have men greatly lived until they were possessed by some convictions for which they were willing to die? When Paul declared, "He who through faith is righteous shall live," he was not thinking of faith as an inherited treasure, a sort of ancestral heirloom to be protected and preserved and worn on state occasions, like a piece of jewelry. No! In the New Testament, faith is something to be fought for and won. It is the reality which is the reward of struggle. It is the refined gold which has withstood the furnace fire consuming the dross.

Lent is a pulpit from which forever is proclaimed: Faith is a risk, a venture, a gamble. Absolute certainty is not faith. Whoever wrote the Letter to the Hebrews knew that. Listen to what it says: "By faith Abraham . . . went out, not knowing where he was to go." He took a chance with God. By faith Moses chose to identify his future with a horde of slaves who were planning a dash for freedom. It was a dubious venture, but he took that risk rather than settle down among the princely luxuries of Egypt. Abraham and Moses, and those other heroic figures sketched on the vast canvas of the centuries, proved their faith by fighting for it.

An old hymn sounds a timeless truth in the line, "Sure, I must fight if I would reign." A battle is always a venture. We revel now in our democratic faith. How easy it is in some great company, with a comfortable surge of patriotism, to pledge allegiance to the flag! But how often dim is the realization that somebody fought for the faith whose glories we now simply recite.

The American Revolution was a great gamble. The faith of the Founding Fathers involved high adventure. Instead of being memorialized by the capital city that bears his honored name and by a monument that leaps skyward to tell of the virtues of his character, George Washington might have been hanged as a traitor to the mother country. We owe our free institutions of government and religion to those who were fierce fighters for their faith.

Safety first is never the mark of true knighthood. When we think of the insecurity and jeopardy that every chapter about fighters depicts, some present tendencies become very disturbing. History shouts that when any system makes its goal comfort and convenience and bleaches out adventure, it is doomed. Christianity began not as an ivory tower of escape, not as an opiate for life's pangs and pain, but as a great adventure.

In the New Testament, faith is a matter of personal venturesomeness. It is a personal relationship to the Christ who said and says, "Follow me." That means that faith is not preservative; it is creative. It is not just a set of assumed and assured finalities; it means daring new sallies into the unknown. Faith is not a retreat into supposed citadels; it is an open road to new adventure.

Too often there have been those who endeavored to take a religion that is a revolution and turn it into a refuge. The Christ of the Passion is saying: "He that saves his life shall lose it. He that loses his life—that is, risks it—for my sake, shall keep it until life eternal."

That faith is a venture in which we invest everything we have and are, and we do it without guaranteed returns. It means launching argosies of hope across unchartered seas. It may be that we must go to our Calvary and mount our cross without knowing whether it will bring us shame or fame. But remember, when darkness fell over a dead Man hanging on a cross, his relentless enemies thought that, at last, the Disturber was utterly defeated. Even his friends agreed that he had lost his gallant fight. However, in the words of G. A. Studdert-Kennedy:

> Before the westering sun went down,
> Crowning that day with its crimson crown
> He knew that He had won.

Getting Along by
Doing Without

JUST a turn of the knob and, without knocking, there troops noisily into our homes a procession of barkers, each in excited, staccato tones extolling the superlative wares for sale inside his particular commercial tent. We are deluged with assertions that infallible tests have proved that to be happy, healthy, wealthy, and wise, we simply cannot do without the boons offered.

Our so-called civilization is cluttered, cumbered, and almost smothered with things. Now for the 101 devices that save time, decrease drudgery, and increase comfort, we raise a Te Deum of gratitude.

When John Ruskin journeyed across England in a horse-drawn stagecoach as a spectacular protestation against what the railroads were doing to mar the rural landscape of the lovely shires, he did not turn back the smoking engines by one puff. No one can help his day by just berating it. Today is always the point of no return. The horse-and-buggy age has gone forever. For better or for worse, we must accept our physical universe.

The cure for the ills of our mechanical age is not in the direction of Clifford Gessler's "The Reasonable Life." He would escape our gadget-ridden, ambition-driven, and fear-haunted modern slavery by copying the ways and attitudes of the relaxed people of the South Sea Islands, among whom he long lived.

He longs for the gentleness, relaxation, and reasonableness that are grown in that tropical garden. At Forty-second and

Broadway he sighs wistfully for the palm-fringed atolls where the code of living forbids hoarding, prohibits the laying up of treasure that cannot be shared, and where none is allowed to go hungry.

However, the delectable life under these languid palms cannot be uprooted and set down in the midst of our competitive rush, which seeks to pile up riches, to gather into barns and banks in the mad race to get on in the world, and which all the time may be wearing out our tired hearts, breaking our taut nerves, and starving our neglected souls.

How keenly multitudes long for the beautiful Isle of Somewhere was indicated by the phenomenal sale of *Peace of Mind*, in which a Hebrew rabbi pointed the way to still waters. It is made clear, in that golden volume and in all other valid guides to a tranquil mind, that the gate is narrow and that superfluous baggage may bar one from the high road. The push of progress, the pressure of propaganda, and the drive of mass production have not enriched the quality of culture. They have robbed us of peace and poise, filled our hospitals with neurotics and the streets of our cities with hurrying people who have forgotten even the grace of courtesy and have lost the sublime secret that "to give is to live." As an observer of our Main Streets has put it, "They jerk their way through hectic days with an acceleration beyond the capacity of the human spirit to endure."

Surely the call of this decisive day is away from know-how to know-why and know-where. It is a summons to halt—to be still—and enter into refreshing realization of the things we can get along without.

The story is told of a woman who went to a shopping district of her city bent on reveling in the glittering exhibition of things. She had ten dollars to spend on anything she wanted badly enough to lure the cash from her pocketbook. On the way home, with a strange light in her eyes she exclaimed to a friend, "I've had the most wonderful shopping trip I ever remember!"

Looking with curiosity at the shopper's empty hands, the friend asked, "What did you buy?"

"Nothing," was the reply. "That's what makes it so marvelous! I couldn't find what I had in mind to purchase. But, somehow, as I looked in a lot of shop windows, I got all steamed up about the enormous number of things I am really better off without."

That was a greater victory than Thoreau's at Walden Pond, as he lived with no tempting things in sight. All real triumphs are won not out of the world, but in the world. The way to get a lift from shopping is to look gleefully at the things one can do without—especially if, with the money you haven't spent, you can therefore make an added contribution toward answering your own daily prayer, "Thy kingdom come."

Life opens into vaster amplitudes when there flashes the emancipating vision that we can get along without things whose possession sentences other people to poverty. We certainly can get along without cushioning our own lives with the things that impoverish our own panting hearts. We can do without anything that keeps us from seeing, feeling, helping, and growing, lest we be among those who with loaded arms yet "with hobbled feet and blinded eyes grope down a narrow gorge, and call it life."

Can it be that we Americans are paying far too much for things that we can do without?

Frozen Melody

THERE is a lovely story not woven out of fiction but growing out of one of the expeditions to the south polar regions a generation ago. The vessel involved was the good ship *Fram*. In those days the hardy boats battering their way through the ice barriers were not heated as are the more modern carriers. On this adventurous trip one of the party took along his pet canary. The cage was hung in the open, chilly space into which all the cramped cabins opened. In that frigid atmosphere one might assume that the little feathered creature, exiled from its sunny native clime, refused to sing canary songs.

However, to the unbounded delight of those men entombed by white walls of ice, just the opposite was true. As one of them put it when he returned: "Our golden chorister never sang with more gayety and abandon than when the ship was in the midst of that vast ice expanse. He sang as though his little throat would burst, even near the South Pole." This canary's melody was not frozen in that zero world.

We were all told in nursery days about a king's party involving singing birds. On this occasion the temperature was as torrid as a baked pie. However, the birds cooperated in the festive arrangements, for when the pie was opened the four and twenty blackbirds all began to sing—doubtless to the royal delight. At least, there was no danger of frozen melody spoiling that kingly feast.

Several years after the close of the Civil War, General U. S. Grant came to the beginning of his second term as president.

The inaugural ball was staged in a huge 330-foot structure erected for the occasion in Judiciary Square. The interior decorations were spectacular. A unique feature in preparation for the gala night was the placing of several hundred caged canaries inside the great hall. These feathered songsters were counted on to lift rapturous notes, soaring even above the chords of the Marine Band's salute: "Hail to the Chief!" But the best-laid plans of mice and men often go awry.

At Grant's inaugural ball not one canary added its expected warble to the presidential oratorio. Each of those hundreds of birds was utterly mute, because every member of that yellow-surpliced choir was utterly miserable. The trouble was that every contingency had been thought of except the weather, and on that March day the temperature was down to near zero. That polar setting stifled songs. The notes anticipated from the shivering canaries died in their throats. Both birds and dancers were victims of what one called a "frosty horror."

The songless canaries, with their padlocked throats and frozen melody, suggest a parable of the ways of men. To every life come solemn inaugurals, as tasks and duties confront each person with their weight and challenge. In work well done song comes through sacrifice. But, just as we are stimulated or depressed by the air we breathe, so we are uplifted or repressed by the atmosphere accompanying the personalities whom we know and who come into proximity with our own lives.

We cannot meet some men without going away from them with our ideals a little tarnished and our faith a little more faint. From others we never part without a sense of increased hope and courage. They are like an elixir such as Matthew Arnold described his father's presence to be when he came to any dispirited group. Such men put warmth into the air; yet, like Moses, they know not that their faces shine. What they bring cannot be analyzed. But the atmosphere they carry makes us believe more deeply in ourselves and in our kind. They bring out the song.

How the carping critics tore to shreds Walt Whitman's book of poems, *Leaves of Grass!* It was his ruling passion to lift the song of democracy, but some saw in his rhapsody only lewdness. They missed the loveliness, forgetting that a lark may start its ascent to the sky even from a barnyard. The blast from the critics so chilled the spirit of the "good gray poet" that he thought he would not attempt to sing again; perhaps he was a frog, and not a thrush! One day he actually threw his book out the window, as if it were a winged creature frozen to death. Then came a letter from Ralph Waldo Emerson with this assurance: "I greet you at the beginning of a great career." That message exchanged the chill for a thrill. And in the atmosphere warmed by understanding Walt Whitman sang on.

And so there are those who come not with a light but with a blight, who bring not a song but a sob. Their sour attitudes stifle notes in throats that in more genial air would burst into joyous melody. There are others, radiant spirits, who bring the balmy breath of spring whenever they come near. Said an admirer of William Morris Hunt, "He lighted up everything he touched."

There are many inaugurals, in addition to presidential ones, when men turn to heavy tasks and great responsibilities determined to give the best that is in them and to fail neither God nor man. When we are tempted to sit in the seat of the scornful and hurl the cynic's ban, let us remember that it is not much of an achievement to be a close relative of Scrooge, who carried his own freezing temperature with him until the spirit of Christmas thawed him out. Inaugural hopes never will sing in the freezing atmosphere of unreasoning prejudice, blind partisanship, and carping criticism. To change the nipping air so that one silent songster, huddled in the cold, will throw back its head and pour out notes of liquid joy because you came near is the richest satisfaction earth can give.

A thermometer simply registers the temperature; a thermostat can change it. Blessed is the man who warms the frosty air, whose kindling words keep men on their feet and call forth the cadence of singing birds.

On Omitting
Flowers

"PLEASE OMIT FLOWERS" is a request often is-
sued when arrangements are announced for what usually is
called a funeral service. In life's darkest hours, when it seems
as a dear one goes from our sight and side that life has tumbled
in, this strange new directive puts a taboo on the Creator's
petaled masterpieces, which can say nameless things that no
human lips can utter.

From where comes this incongruous suggestion? Omit flowers—in the Valley of the Shadow, when every yearning impulse
is struggling vainly to express feelings that are too deep for
words! Then it is that flowers offer wings to affection, appreciation, and consolation, to wistful memories and assurances
of sympathy.

Of course, carping critics of any custom may suspect the
aroma of commercialism in the slogan admittedly coined by
vendors of blooms: "Say it with flowers." But alas for the one
who in so fragrant a phrase detects only the ring of the florist's
cash register. In "Say it with flowers" there stretch enchanting
vistas of sacramental beauty like the glory of a garden or the
shimmer of moonlight on a silvery sea.

A choice friend, here no more, whose spiritual apprehensions
found radiant kinship in flowers as he pondered a posy's secret
for entering the sacristy of another's felicity or pain, left us
this verbal bouquet:

The enterprising florist does not attempt to suggest what you shall
say. That is your part of the enterprise. His to supply the
vocabulary, so to speak; yours to select the particular words required for your message. Indeed, your floral gift can say things
of exquisite delicacy and tender meaning for the expression of

which a dictionary leaves you impotent. Heart-meanings conveyed by flowers become prismatic, whose white light breaks into a perfect shower of crimson, violet and gold.

Yet some boldly propose to blow out all the floral candles on the high altar of grief—to bar all that glory from the place of mourning and remembrance—when the daughters of music are brought low! No Trespassing signs are set up against the consoling presence of the splendor that had captured the very being of Oliver Wendell Holmes when he declared, "The Amen of nature is always a flower." Some unnamed constable dares to forbid the entry of the gay loveliness which banished his gloom, as Emerson gratefully remarks, "Earth laughs in flowers."

In a poet's rapture Walt Whitman cried: "A morning glory at my window satisfies me more than the metaphysics of books." And it was Tennyson, with a tiny blossom held in his hand, who soliloquized that if man could tell all that is mirrored there he would know what God and man are. In his "Hymn to the Flowers," Horace Smith pointed to their inspiring ministry in unforgettable lines:

> Were I in churchless solitudes remaining,
> Far from all voice of teachers and divines,
> My soul would find, in flowers of God's ordaining,
> Priests, sermons, shrines!

In the midst of such a Hallelujah Chorus, lifting to highest heaven a paean of gratitude for the tint of the tiniest flower, how impertinent appears a notice with this strange message: "Please omit flowers." What! Bring no symbols of the white flowers of immortality that bloom around the solitude of the grave? Omit flowers when gathered friends come to hear the triumphal assurance that death is but a portal to another room in the Father's many-mansioned house? No flowers as emblems whispering of the virtues and graces that made the earthly life of the one who has finished the course like a garden of the Lord?

How bleak and bare the "last rites" can be when there is no loft from which comes the solace of a multicolored, surpliced flower choir in the chapel of death. Oh, to be sure, like any other hallowed ritual, defiling hands may turn it all into a vulgar display of pagan extravagance. But there is an old proverb warning against emptying the baby out with the bath. A remedy for excesses which prescribes that flowers be eliminated when and where they are needed most, savors of the ruthless iconoclast.

But listen, says one with a cold gleam in his eye. Why not give the money spent for flowers to some humanitarian cause? How piously realistic! The undertones of that proposition are suspiciously like the disciples' suggestion when a woman poured a precious ointment on the head of the Master she adored. The miserly instincts of the disciples tried to measure the sunbeam of this fragrant deed with a monetary yardstick: "Why this waste?" This could have been sold and the proceeds given to the Jerusalem Community Chest! But Jesus, who cared supremely for the poor, said: "Why do you trouble the woman? . . . She has done it to prepare me for burial." He was not in favor of omitting flowers.

If the injunction of the disciples, omit ointment, had prevailed, this ointment would not have been used as balm for the wounds of the poor. And those who have looked fairly percentage-wise into the situation today report that omitting flowers where their potent ministry is needed most benefits the needy scarcely at all.

Funerals and memorial services are not the only occasions when the sign Omit Flowers needs to be carefully inspected and appraised. Gruff Thomas Carlyle sobbed bitterly as he bowed at his wife's grave. He felt that through the years he had omitted the flowers of praise and affection. The sin of omission was now like a sword through his soul. With gnawing regret, he muttered: "O Mary, I loved you all the while! If I had only told you." Alas for flowers that never arrive until after the undertaker has been summoned.

If we would practice the simple rule of being a little kinder, a little more thoughtful, we would escape the prickling regret of these searching lines:

> It isn't the thing you do, dear;
>   It's the thing you leave undone,
> Which gives you a bit of heartache
>   At the setting of the sun.

Every week we rub elbows with fellow pilgrims whose hearts are famished, hungering unwittingly, perhaps, for a crust of encouragement. Some "Well done," some gracious word from us might come with the beauty and fragrance of a flower. But too often we do not say it.

What a calling—to be florists in the realm of praise and fragrant words that keep men on their feet! Remember Tolstoi's beggar who, in the thrill of a salutation that lifted him to the level of brotherhood, forgot even his empty stomach. And never forget, at your peril, that Jesus declared that the final condemnation would be reserved for those who forgot the flowers of mercy and help.

The meanest kind of miser is one who omits the flowers of generous speech. Felicia Hemans penned a verse that might well be entitled "Please Do Not Omit Flowers":

> They speak of hope to the fainting
> heart,
> With a voice of promise they come
> and part;
> They sleep in dust through the wintry
> hours,
> They break forth in glory—
> Bring flowers, bright flowers!

Upstairs

In spite of many examples of modern home building which plan for all domestic life to be lived on one level, the romance of stairways remains. A cultured woman recently was heard to remark: "When stairways disappear something precious goes out of the home."

With bright strands of remembrance stairs are woven into the warp and woof of gracious living. A cherished part of our national heritage consists of stately homes, exuding the aroma of days of yore, whose stairways are artists' dreams of proportion, symmetry, and grace. In the annals of many a family tradition a sweeping stairway is redolent with nostalgic memories as vivid as Longfellow's picture of "The Children's Hour." There the poet captured forever, in eternal youth, the gay trio of merry maidens as they came tripping in the lamplight, descending the broad hall stair with whispered plots and plans to make "a sudden rush from the stairway" and take the poet by surprise.

Such stairs tell not only of jubilant feet descending but of reluctant feet halting in the ascent, with pouting children pleading for some extension of the seemingly cruel parental decree, "Upstairs to bed!"

T. A. Daly has a touching little poem in which he etches a never-to-be-forgotten picture of two dear friends parting after happy, understanding hours by blazing logs. The one is seen mounting the stairs after "farewell" was whispered, leaving the other standing by the hearth, whose flickering light had cast its playful, fitful shadows on both faces. As the one turns to go, a haloed radiance seems to creep upstairs with her, leaving only shadows where she had sat by the dying red embers. Holding a candle to light the way, she disappears at the head of the stairs. The door of an upper room is heard to close. Then the house is very still. The night seems suddenly to grow cold and a chill hand to be laid on the lonely one sitting with bowed head by the faint-glowing ashes. That one, in the presence of the other, had reveled in that winter evening as in a garden of delight; but now—

> Good night! And then your candle's
>   feeble glare
> Went glimmering up the stair.
> For, oh, the summer, warm and bright,
> You conjured in the winter night,
> Went upward with your candlelight,
> Went with you up the stair.

Such a verse is freighted with the pathos of the stairs. That separation is a glowing parable speaking wistfully of those who have ascended stairs to an upper room in mansions above, of the Father's house, leaving disconsolate those who stay behind a while bowed in the sadness of farewell. But in going, such leave a breath of fragrant summer behind; for, before they go up the golden stairs, their flame has touched with fire some other. That is how all the best and the good has defied the corroding years as the living flame has leaped from candle to candle.

The church started when tongues of fire sat upon each of those waiting hearts who had climbed the stairs to an upper room. They found the same Presence which Jacob found as, from his lonely rock in the wilderness, a stairway suddenly spanned the gulf between him and the unseen, while the angels of God ascended and descended. Having caught the flame, those first disciples came down the stairs to enact the wonder of the spreading flame which is the heart of Christianity.

Stairways become symbols of lives that climb—each new day a step to higher levels of thinking and achieving. Blessed is the man who, having ascended one more step and with eyes lifted to others yet to mount, can greet each eventide with the triumphant satisfaction, I have climbed a little higher today! What an epitaph there is on one Alpine slope where a gallant climber met his fate! Where he slipped to his death is a white stone on which are his name and the simple, significant statement: "He died climbing."

There are only two vital divisions among men. The difference between the two is not one of position; it is one of direction. In the one are those who, however high they start, are moving down; in the other, those who, however low they start, are moving up. Toward the place where you will one day stand you are now moving. If you keep on living as you are living now, where will it take you? The answer to that solemn question is not suggested by an escalator, which automatically moves up, but a stairway, up which one climbs. "We build the ladder by which we rise—and mount to its summit, round by round."

There is an inspiring story of a stairway of service that starts in the Southland. The climber of those stairs was once a hillbilly lad, named Carpenter, whose childhood was as hard as the rocks of his native South Carolina mountains. One day he was taken to a city where he beheld the wonders of trains and lights and crowded streets. He felt the urge to climb from his lowly beginnings. To his joy it was arranged that he should live with an uncle and go to high school. He made friends who believed in him. Teachers recognized his ability. He had the stuff to climb. They offered to send him to college. He was thrilled. With sparkling eyes, he said, "I want to be a doctor!"

He studied hard and came through with high honors. The medical faculty saw a likely candidate for specialization in hospital research. But the young man said, "Thank you, no. I appreciate your help and kindness, but I want to go back to my native mountains. There are sick people there who die because they have no doctor." That is where he went and stayed—stayed until he was no longer a young physician, but "old Dr. Carpenter."

The people he served were so poor that they could not pay him in money, but in provisions and feed for his horse. He lived in two rooms over the village store, with a stairway outside. At the foot of the stairs was a shingle: Dr. Carpenter Upstairs.

A morning came when someone climbed those old stairs to get his friend for another case of need, and found that during the night the doctor had answered a higher call "Upstairs." People came from miles and miles, in stunned sorrow. They laid him to rest in a box of pine, there in the red earth. One of the group said, "I know just where to get a sign for his headstone." While they waited he ran to the village store and took from the foot of the old stairway the weather-beaten shingle that had directed the sick for many years. While the mourners stood around in breathless silence, he placed it at the head of the old doctor's grave: Dr. Carpenter Upstairs.

There is nothing to do now but to kneel by that sign and pray that for each of us the things that were and the things that are and the things that are to be may form a golden stairway by which we shall mount up, up, up, to our waiting throne and to the inheritance of the saints in light.

Banquet of
Consequences

EVERYBODY, soon or late, sits down to a banquet
of consequences, declared Robert Louis Stevenson in a penetrating comment on life. That suggests the solemn reminder
of the Master Teacher that men cannot expect a harvest of
grapes from thorns or figs from thistles. At the banquet of consequences to which every person and every nation and every
civilization sooner or later sits down, the cook is "cause,"
and the menu prepared in the kitchen of thoughts and deeds
is "effect." The Creator has put us in a universe which is not
whimsical or haphazard, but which is all law. Confronting
lawbreakers on the highways of God's world are angels with
flaming swords; and no traffic tickets can be "fixed."

On the banquet-of-consequences table there often are things
bitter and sour which set teeth on edge, and at this table one
is often compelled to eat his own words and actions. All the
great religions stress the truth that there is only one way to
make the inevitable banquet of consequences palatable and
devoid of wormwood and gall. And that is to find and accept
the will of God. The deepest secret of a victorious life is to
move in the direction in which the kindly light of the divine
purpose is leading.

Long ago Augustine put in one sentence what dozens of
modern volumes, which purport to point the way to peace of
mind, are trying to say. In that handful of words is the quintessence of all wisdom: "In his will is our peace."

William E. Gladstone spoke as a true statesman and sage
when he declared that the height of wisdom in any one day is

to find out where God Almighty is going in the next fifty years, and then to move out in that direction. It was because England's grand old man believed and practiced that high art that he could say with unruffled assurance when his reform bill, even then long overdue, was defeated: "You can't fight against the future. The great social forces which move onwards in their might and majesty and which the tumult of our debate does not for a moment impede or disturb—those great social forces are against you; they are marshaled on our side." That was the utterance of a statesman, not a time-serving politician.

By faith Gladstone was living in a later hour, when enraged and outraged justice would say to those who had gloated over some temporary victory, "The banquet of consequences is ready; dinner is served." And so it came to pass—and not to the delight of the taste buds of those who, defying consequences, had prepared the bill of fare.

History fairly shouts that in the banquet of consequences Louis XIV insured Robespierre, the blindness of the Russian czar brought Lenin, and the inhumanity of human slavery led on to the American Civil War. Confidence, never dimmed by hours of seeming defeat, grows out of the fundamental belief that God always is on the side of those who minister to great human needs. That has ever been the guiding star of those who have really prayed, "Thy kingdom come, thy will be done."

The heart of Abraham Lincoln's religion was to be sure that he was moving in the direction of God's intent. When some partisans were insisting on putting a sanctimonious halo around what they wanted to happen and claiming the proud distinction of having the Almighty himself as an ally on their side, Lincoln, with a moral insight which, like lightning, illuminated a dark landscape, had the perfect comment when he drawled, "Well, I am not so much concerned as to whether God is on my side as I am whether I am on God's side."

The German kaiser was not the first, nor the last, to raise the banner of "Me and God" over aggressive schemes that never rightly could claim the blessing of the God of goodness, mercy, and justice. What happened to him at the banquet of consequences, and later tyrants in Germany and Italy, history has recorded; and as far as other autocrats are concerned, on those tables are piled the grapes of wrath. The last entry has not yet been made.

Now that the supreme test of America has come and we face the record of the past, we must be stripped of our illusions and our false pride. We must be purged of greed and injustice. We must not only see the needs of America, and the Americas, and Europe; we must also feel the suppressed yearning of a billion retarded members of the human family in Asia and Africa. Somehow we must see through their eyes the meager lot that hitherto, partly through the selfishness of the West, they have been doomed to endure. We must be on their side as far as their legitimate strivings are concerned if we are to be on the side of the God of all the earth, the Father of all mercies who even now is thundering to entrenched and callous privilege, "Let my people go!"

The banquet-of-consequences table at which we now sit is suggested by what Dean Inge, who died in 1954, warned us of years back, when he said from the lofty pedestal of St. Paul's Cathedral that the chief danger of the white man is his arrogant contempt for other races. Western nations today are reaping the whirlwind of resentment among the native peoples of the East because they have too often sowed the wind of selfish exploitation. The yellow and brown people of the Orient now are demanding that the boasted "whiteness" of the West be expressed in international and interracial living to match the reality and sincerity of the Christ whom the East gave to the world.

Only if in this sense we are on God's side, the side of his children everywhere who are made in his image, can we really make a prayer out of the appealing request "God bless America." That never must mean that we call on God to return to our democracy and bless it; but, rather, that together we shall cause our democracy to return to God and be blessed.

Where God's will lies is not the vague question many have assumed it is. Always, that will is identified with the welfare of people. That is what the Bible means when it says that the stars in their courses fought against Sisera. It is a vain thing to claim that the stars are with us. It is everything if we are with the stars.

Said an effusive young lady to a great theologian and

preacher at one of Oxford's colleges, "Do tell me what you think about God." To which the great scholar replied: "That, my dear young lady, is a rather unimportant question. The only thing that signifies is what God thinks about me."

Individuals and nations need have no fear of the banquet of consequences if at last it can be said, in the words of the Old Testament, "He brought me to the banqueting house,/and his banner over me was love." If love is the autocrat of that dining table, all will be well.

The Factors of
Destiny

YEARS ago a noted speaker delivered a lecture in a college chapel. He was a famous and brilliant orator. Most of what was uttered on that occasion has long ago faded from memory, but the opening sentences were destined to be written indelibly on the mind of a sophomore student who heard them. The ripening and revealing experiences of life have but burnished the truth they proclaim.

One sentence flames in letters of light. The man with the message paused dramatically after being introduced and then began: "The other day I met a man who said to me, 'I suppose you will agree that the factors of destiny are two, heredity and environment.' I replied, 'I will agree to nothing of the kind.' " Now comes the deathless sentence: " 'The factors of destiny are not two, but four: Heredity, environment, self and God.' "

One cannot ignore the first factor of this quartet. As we start on the adventure of keeping the date with destiny, we have to acknowledge, as Oliver Wendell Holmes put it: "We are not private carriages. We are omnibuses, and the passengers we carry are our own ancestors." Through the whole realm of living things runs the great law of inheritance. Men do not gather grapes from thorns, nor figs from thistles. By some subtle, mysterious process one life is able to incarnate itself in the tendencies of its offspring. For instance, the wanderlust of the gypsy is in his blood; he just cannot help himself.

Along all the lines of his personality—physical, mental, and moral—man derives from his past. A biographer of Charles Darwin said: "A great man springs from an ancestry competent to produce him." Yes, without question, one of the factors of destiny is heredity.

And who can doubt that not just what we are but where we are colors the picture? Environment does count. We do not strive in a vacuum. John Bunyan's *Pilgrim's Progress,* a book of the centuries, belongs with the classics. Its spiritual insights are as valid today as when, in jail, the Bedford tinker wrote his graphic portrayal. We might assume that such a man, who has spoken to the ages about spiritual verities, must have had a godly early environment. But listen to him: "From a child I had few equals in cursing, blaspheming and lying. So settled and rooted was I in these things that they became as a second nature to me. I was the very ringleader of the youths who kept me company in all manner of vice and ungodliness." That is what surroundings did to Bunyan in his early years.

In the early Christian centuries the so-called pillar saints spent their days perched far up above the ground in order that they would not be exposed to evil enticements. But no pillar saint could be lifted above himself. Always a vital factor in destiny is the self.

Heredity may determine the form in which temptations shall come to a man, whether lust or duplicity or greed; but the result of the temptation rests with the man himself. Heredity may fix the place of a battle, but not the outcome.

Years ago, at a certain gathering a well-known man read a paper on heredity. Present on that occasion was one who later attained eminence in his profession. That one, then a young man, was called out of the room before the message ended. After he had gone a scrap of paper was found on the table by which he had been sitting. On it he had scribbled these words: "What he is saying about heredity is true. And mine is all pure devil." But the young man who left that comment determined that his foot should be set upon the devil's neck, and remain there. Long years after, the very man who read that paper on heredity said of the other man: "With many a tendency to base living he walks the earth everywhere useful and deservedly honored."

A widely read commentator once called attention to the fact that Julius Rosenberg and Dr. Jonas Salk were raised in identical early surroundings in congested sections of New York City. Both came from Jewish families, and both went to the same college. Each made science his lifework. Julius Rosenberg died in the electric chair a traitor to his country, as despised in American history as Benedict Arnold. But the name of Jonas Salk probably is destined, because of his indefatigable research, to take its place with the few immortal names who have saved mankind from the fatalities of a dreaded scourge. Both of these men, coming from the same surroundings, had to reckon with self.

However, the factors of destiny are not three, but four: heredity, environment, self, and God. The prophet Ezekiel, more than five hundred years before Christ, gave to mankind the charter of liberty for which we are fighting today. He determined to stop the mouths of men who were pleading the sins of their fathers to explain their own wrongdoing. The prophet met the excuse of heredity and environment with a great and universal truth, as spoken to him by God. Here are the momentous words: "Behold, all souls are mine." That is to say, every individual soul is related to God. We do draw from the past, but that which we derive from the past is not the whole of it. We derive also from God. Every individual soul is linked directly with the Creator. We are rooted in God.

Robert Louis Stevenson wrestled with heredity. He had a weak body. He faced the problem of environment, changing from the chill hills of his Scottish home to sun-kissed southern islands. He insisted on being master of his fate, with his dauntless self always in the saddle. However, there was one other thing. He tells it thus: "I came about like a well-handled ship. There stood at the wheel that unknown steersman whom we call God." In God the other factors of destiny came to their fruition.

Back to
Valley Forge

THIS IS George Washington speaking from Valley Forge. He is pleading to the United States Congress to hurry supplies for his twelve thousand hungry, sick, cold, tattered, and poorly armed troops. Poignantly Washington cries: "To see men without clothing to cover their nakedness—without blankets to lie down—their marks traced by the blood from their feet as they go through the frost and snow without shoes —and yet submitting to it without complaint, is proof of patience and obedience which in my opinion can scarcely be paralleled."

Yet in that terrible situation only a few miles from Valley Forge hundreds of Tories openly became cheerleaders for the British taskmasters. There were also cheap, ambitious politicians, detractors, and outside traitors among Washington's inner circle of advisers.

A well-known clergyman, who had acted as chaplain at the Continental Congress and offered daily prayer for the success of the daring venture, proved a quitter. In the name of patriotism and religion he urged Washington to come to his senses and realize the impossibility of victory. He strongly advised the commander to make the best bargain the Redcoats would accept, to call off the rebellion with its horrible cost. Washington's indignant reply to this turncoat was colder than the Valley Forge winter. Yet it is no exaggeration to say that the Revolution was really won at Valley Forge during those hundred winter days of torture in 1777/78.

Listen now to another voice from that same spot almost two hundred years later. This is another general, Dwight D.

Eisenhower, speaking from Valley Forge to two hundred million Americans from the fifty states of the Union: "We meet on this place to rededicate ourselves to the dream that is America. It is difficult to avoid giving away to emotion so intense as to still the tongue and to leave any American silently grateful, humble, reverent. For here Washington staged and won the greatest fight of his fighting career. For here is our Spiritual Temple."

This great general, who commanded the mightiest army ever to challenge tyranny, is saying that you Americans are the leaders in perfecting the vision that sustained Washington in Valley Forge. With all the valor of old, you must hurl defiance to all who would destroy the American dream—in a crisis out of which our land can emerge only through clear thinking, loyalty, courage, and stamina—a crisis through which America can and will survive every threat and every challenge.

Our Republic stands here today in plain sight of the great historic jubilee of its 200th anniversary in 1976. Thomas Jefferson, the third president, whose hands wrote the immortal Declaration, left word that he desired no epitaph on his grave at Monticello except one noting that he had helped to build the educational monument at the University of Virginia.

Now the physical form of Dwight D. Eisenhower, the thirty-fourth president of the United States, rests in the heartland of America at his loved Abilene. He asked for no titles, no military or academic or political office. He vowed to preserve this land of the free through his effort for many years under Freedoms Foundation. Here is his benediction to all America and to all the world: "I want in this public testimony to testify to the glowing idea embodied in Freedoms Foundation of Valley Forge and to my conviction that the great struggle of our time is one of the spirit. It is a struggle for the heart and soul of man—not merely for material property or power. It is a contest for the belief—the very innermost soul—of the human being! In other words, our form of government has no sense unless it is founded in a deeply felt religious faith."

Here forever is the Eisenhower epitaph. No wonder that increasing millions—yes millions—of American citizens are united with no profit, no political plan, and no sectarianism, but only the basic truth of our inheritance, to pass on intact to succeeding generations the fundamental creed, "I believe in God and in man and in human freedom." That credo alone—

> Gives the priceless gift of freedom
> For the home, the church, the school
> For the open door of manhood
> In a land the people rule.

The processes of national disintegration are so dreadfully at work in the world today that the regiments of righteous must march in a conquering crusade with banners floating and with trumpets sounding for America to return anew to the spirit of Valley Forge. Freedoms Foundation in this imperiled day is not asking freemen what they want from the Republic, but rather what they are eager to give so that liberty may not perish from the earth. The motto in such an age does not concern what Americans are against, but what they are for. This inspiring channel of pure democracy under the Stars and Stripes is asking the question of questions in this grim day: "Do you live in a democracy or does democracy live in you?" It is not for demonstrators, rabble-rousers, and sidewalk orators to parrot, "We've got to get rid of the Establishment," knowing that what they are so hostile against is the only thing that today demands and preserves a semblance of order in our society.

There are some good people in these days who are so badly frightened that they have almost reached the point of making a mockery of their dreams. But this is not a time to panic and stand before a mirror mesmerized by one's own misery. Salvation is the return to Valley Forge, in spite of sabotage and subversion, to the eternal values we hold dear. Issues in which God and truth have a stake will abide. Perhaps there may not always be an England, but there will always be a kingdom of God. As a great American, one of my dearest friends, who passed away not long ago, said as he referred to Freedoms Foundation, "Never forget a book is more than pulp and ink, a house is more than timber and plaster, and history is more than Hitler." Hope is in the hands of men who keep faith in God. Against them the gates of hell cannot prevail.

While addressing his first State of the Union pronouncement to the joint session of Congress, President Nixon declared, "More important than legislative programs we need spiritual and moral leadership which no programs for material progress can satisfy—a sense of destiny." And even before that, Woodrow Wilson, in his last address on the "Road Away from Revolution," warned: "The sum of the whole matter is that our civilization cannot survive materially unless it is redeemed spiritually. Only thus can discontent be driven out and all the shadows lifted from the road ahead." Thus will all the shadows of counterrevolution be lifted from the road ahead as all true patriots are mobilized at Valley Forge.

Seven Miles
from Sin

ACROSS the centuries men have tried to get away from evil. They have thought that if they could put miles between themselves and some temptation, they would be safe. They have assumed that if there was a distance between themselves and some vice threatening to seduce them, they might obtain the victory.

The pillar saints in the early Christian centuries spent lonely years away from alluring temptations of the common earth and of sinful men. They sought perfection in elevated isolation. Some who craved the satisfactions of a holy life fled into monastery cells to escape defilement. But to choose separation as the chief guarantee of saintliness is to rob the good life of most of its significance. Christianity has to do not with goodness out of the world, but with goodness in it. Christ's wish for his disciples was that they might be in the world but not of it.

The greatest fallacy regarding sin is that it has mostly to do with geography. The final battle for character is not to be won by any quarantine regulations. A small college under the control of an extremely fundamentalist sect advertised that its campus was seven miles from any known form of sin. This ad would, of course, have its appeal for parents troubled by being told that most college campuses are seedbeds of evil. This college said: "Avoid that danger by sending your children to us. We are seven miles from sin."

A highly intelligent citizen, deeply concerned about modern college life, commented on that announcement thus: "Seven miles from sin! That would be a good trick if you could do it. There are few things I would be unwilling to do in order to get seven miles from sin. But because sin is in my heart, and no one is able to tell me how to get seven miles from myself, the whole idea is fallacious."

In a well-known publication some time ago there appeared an article entitled "The Hound of Heaven." It told the tragedy of a famous cartoonist. He was a brilliant man and greatly gifted. And, as the world counts success, he reached the top. But at the height of his fame he committed suicide, leaving behind a letter that has been called one of the greatest sermons ever preached. Here is a part of it:

I have run from wife to wife, from house to house and from country to country, in a ridiculous effort to escape from myself. In so doing I am very much afraid that I have brought a great deal of unhappiness to those who have loved me. No one thing is responsible for this, except myself.

He tried to put a thousand times seven miles between himself and his sin. But sin kept up with him, as it did with Paul, who declared in a classic confession: "Wretched man that I am! Who will deliver me from this body of death?" Well, Paul found, as life's conquerors have always found, that the secret is not to keep seven miles away from sinful enticements. The secret is to carry about at the center of one's personality a beauty that will outshine the phosphorescent rottenness of any evil thing.

In Shakespeare's *Othello,* Iago says of Cassio, "He hath a daily beauty in his life that makes me ugly." That daily beauty of heart is the best antidote against any ugliness that may assail the soul. It suggests a purity that does not feel safe just because it has fled from some corruption festering seven miles away.

Away up in the highlands of Scotland there is a hunting lodge which, because of something that came to pass there, is a mecca for travelers. One day many years ago, a number of guests were dining in a newly decorated room. In an attempt to open a bottle of soda one of the company splashed its contents over the lovely wall near which he was standing. The beauty of the design was ruined. All present, deploring the accident, hoped that when the liquid had dried no stain would remain. But, alas, it did not turn out that way. The defacement appeared to be permanent. There was an unsightly splotch stretching almost from floor to ceiling. The host did not attempt to hide his chagrin and resentment at what had happened to the wall.

The guests departed, greatly regretting this anticlimax to a gay occasion. They went off to leave widening miles between them and the ruined wall. But there was one man who did not go with them. He stayed behind and sat for a long while studying the blotch. Then he went to work with the whole expanse of the wall as his canvas. He began with crayon and charcoal, and finished with oil paints. With deft, bold strokes he changed the brown stains into rugged highland rocks. Over the rocks he depicted a leaping cataract. Where the stain was darkest he painted a glorious highland deer entering the rushing waters, as it was pursued by hunters seen in the background.

Who was it who thus stayed at the soiled spot and changed stains to splendor? It was Sir Edwin Landseer, famed for his paintings of landscapes and animals. An almost constant procession now enters that lodge to see this wondrous thing.

This is the victory that overcomes the world: not to leave evil unchanged, seven or seventy miles away; but to bring beauty out of ugliness and goodness out of evil. The Hebrew prophet Ezekiel wrote these words of the Lord God: "On the day that I cleanse you from all your iniquities, I will cause the cities to be inhabited. . . ."

The city is a saner residence for a good man than a religious retreat. A real saint does not seek sanctified seclusion and pious solitude, but the secular world and the street.

Length and
Strength

THE final problem of life has to do with length and strength. Collapse is sure in any realm if extension goes on without regard to intention and direction.

Long ago a wise prophet formulated a timeless principle. He enunciated a law that is as valid for our speeding, jet-plane, skyscraper age as it was for his nomadic, tent-dwelling day. That ancient law of the tent is: When you lengthen the cords, you must strengthen the stakes. That is not just the law of the tent. It is the law of a cottage or a cathedral, a city or a civilization. It warns that if you go on majoring in length to the neglect of strength, you are heading for calamity and catastrophe.

Trust in the external spread of the tents of physical power, greedy profits, and exciting pleasure, rather than in the strengthened stakes of inner integrity and discipline, is America's direst peril. This is the deliberate judgment of a startling number of leaders whose pulpits are set up in colleges, magazines, popular newspaper columns, and even in Chamber of Commerce conclaves; yes, and in many modern novels also, which, with bitter, disillusioned pessimism and haunting fear, depict creaking canvas with the supporting stakes bending and breaking. It is apparent that the chief woes of our tottering civilization grow out of a pathetic, tragic trust in length without strength, in goods without good, in political activities rather than ethical sanctities.

It has been suggested by a keen student of our times that the principal words in today's vocabulary are words of action, such as *aggressive, progressive, dynamic, vigor;* and that, looking at the picture of modernity, no one would be reminded of such words as *poise, balance, peace, steadfastness, stability.* Then this significant and unrefutable statement is made: "Anyone who knows either biography or history must see that one of the primary tests of character is the ability to increase staunchness as you extend strength."

Who can doubt that in our inventive era, characterized by expansion and extension, the ropes of material and scientific advance have been enormously let out? A century ago, we are told, salesmen offered to the average man only about two hundred different articles. Today, with all the blandishments of modern salesmanship and the high-powered hucksters of radio and television, the average man is urged to put his money on the counter for many thousands of things.

But what about the moral and spiritual stakes to support this vast, expansive canvas? The frightening figures of crime and youth delinquency cry to high heaven that in our expanding, gadget-fascinated day the upholding stakes have been weakened, rather than strengthened. Certainly the parental and community stakes have been allowed to rot to an alarming degree. Great universities, once centered in religion, have become largely secularized. The president of Harvard agreed with Rufus M. Jones that the shrinkage of religion on the part of both professors and students in institutions of higher learning is tragic for the cause of education itself and for the welfare of the nation.

That great New England nursery of culture and learning is revitalizing its Divinity School, bringing for its strengthening dedicated dollars and richly endowed scholars and prophets. All this is being done on the assumption that the fundamentals of successful living are rooted in the unseen and the eternal. This reversal of emphasis is a welcome and heartening antidote for the blighting belief that has seeped in, that the future is not with churches but with laboratories, not with prophets but with scientists, not with piety but with efficiency.

From the cornucopia of modern inventions have poured magic things making for comfort and convenience, for which we are glad. But the trouble is that comfort frequently is mistaken for civilization. Without proper props the great weight of mere things breaks down life itself. It is that danger to which Edna St. Vincent Millay pointed with alarm as she saw the tremendous energy of this dynamic day constantly pulling the straining ropes out to wider expanses. Strengthen the stakes, she is warning in her lines:

> Above the world is stretched the sky,—
> No higher than the soul is high.
>
> . . . .
> And he whose soul is flat—the sky
> Will cave in on him by and by.

The sky of idealism is caving in on multitudes caught with collapsing stakes in the moral sag of today. With all the magic that surrounds us, we live in a world in which cleverness is counted a higher achievement than cleanliness, and selling shoddy goods or shady propositions more essential than telling the truth.

The trouble is that today we are reaping the bitter harvest of a vicious environment whose chief objective is to make life easier instead of stronger.

"What would you say is the most important thing to broadcast from the housetops in the midst of this complicated world?" was the question asked one of the keenest minds of this generation. Here is his answer: "Emphasis upon expansion must be matched by renewed emphasis upon those spiritual forces which stabilize and fortify men, confirm them in self-control, build moral foundations under them, give tenacity to meet tension and steadfastness to meet strength." There it is! It is that or chaos and collapse.

The recipe of salvation from destruction is: spiritual strength to sustain material length.

The Fetters of
Freedom

FREEDOM without fetters is as dangerous as a
high-powered car without brakes. On any highway, wheels not
under control leave damage, destruction, and death in their
wake. In the modern world of wheels, with tremendous horse-
power behind each revolving circle, there must be a skillful
and diligent will in the driver's seat, able to guide and, if
necessary, to stop any speeding piece of twentieth-century
mechanism. Even with all the specified restraints, abused freedom brings yearly its terrible toll of maimed and slaughtered
innocents and of those who pay the supreme penalty as the
result of their own foolhardiness in disregarding the safety
regulations.

And so it is with all exercise of freedom. Amid all the determination of these days to preserve liberties—amid all the
cries of "We want freedom—hands off our freedom," the
pungent question is, "Freedom for what?" As one has put it,
after all there is no particular virtue in wanting freedom for
itself. Even a fish wants to be free—even free to take the bait
that will end its freedom. Don't imagine that you are a noble
breed just because you want freedom. Always the question
confronts one or a group or a whole people shouting for freedom, "What do you want to do with it?" Are you ready to
accept its inevitable fetters? And the disciplines necessary to
keep it?

While democracy is alerted in perilous times like these against
the slavery of regimentation, it must also be warned against
the thralldom of a liberty selfishly misused. A perverted liberty

may become, as Whittier put it, "the prison of the soul." And the name of that prison is license.

This is an hour for those outside the Iron Curtain to listen while our prized democracy looks boasting free men straight in the eye and asks, "What do you mean by freedom?" What do you propose to do with it? Perhaps you have no right to it. A misnamed freedom standing alone, put into the category of rights rather than responsibilities, divorced from the only things that give it strength and luster, such as justice, truth, loyalty, honor, and brotherhood, may be but an instrument to degrade personality—to murder others or even to commit spiritual suicide.

For those who use what they think of as their freedom to do as they please, to shirk self-discipline, and to yield to self-indulgence, George Bernard Shaw makes one of his characters say to a weak-willed woman who wanted her liberty just to escape the fetters of freedom, "Your native language is the language of Shakespeare and Milton and the Bible; don't sit there crooning like a bilious pigeon."

Whenever amiable and well-meaning people are left to handle their own freedom of choice, what happens so often is suggested by the description a youth gave of his uncle who raised him. This is what that youth in his late teens had to say to a minister: "To my uncle Sundays were nice comfortable days when you had a late breakfast and took a walk along the canal bank while dinner was cooking and then had a snooze in the afternoon and high tea at 5 o'clock."

"Did your uncle ever go to church?" the minister asked.

"Oh, when he felt like it. He seemed to feel like it less and less as he grew older. He used to say he'd attend regularly if only Aunt Flo were a bit better on her feet, and he'd have liked to put more in the collection plate if only he hadn't lost so much in cotton investments."

Then, still thinking of his uncle and of those years when that uncle's home was his, the youth remarked, "What he'd have liked to do was so well-meaning you could hardly call him irreligious, while what he actually did was so little that he interfered with nobody."

Ah, there were flabby and purposeless hands at the wheel of that life! This uncle stands for great numbers whose intentions are honorable, but their performances are mediocre. Their freedom is never harnessed to a cause that puts fetters on certain easy tendencies as stern endeavors head for some compelling objective.

The quintessence of liberty is that one can never be free until he is a captive—taken into custody by something bigger than today, something greater than himself. Those hands of Van Cliburn sweeping the responsive keys with delicate, interpretive touch are free because they have been bound. So it is in every field of art and accomplishment.

Sometimes, because of continued wrong choices, the will itself is weakened and enslaved by easy practices. It is no use standing on some moral eminence of one's own, and telling another to break himself free. The harder one tries, the worse off he is likely to be, like a kitten in a skein of yarn that becomes more entangled the more it struggles.

Instead of fruitless struggle, hope lies in surrendering to a power greater than oneself. There are times when a man is lost unless, acknowledging that he is beaten, he turns himself over to God. One of the great preachers in this generation cried out as he spoke to a crowded cosmopolitan congregation: "I might preach self-control to you till the crack of doom. What you need is a power not your own, and greater than your own, to take hold of your will and renew and strengthen it. On page after page the New Testament proclaims that there is no sin to which we have to surrender, no habit we cannot break, no worthy resolve that is beyond fulfillment."

Whenever I see the heroic figure of William Penn lifted above the crowded ways of Philadelphia, I seem to hear him say again, "Man will either choose to be governed by God or condemn himself to be ruled by tyrants."

The great Greek sage Epictetus uttered a timeless truth as, thinking of the possible thralldom of liberty into which freedom with no bit in its mouth leads, he declared, "No bad man is free."

George Matheson's great hymn captures in two lines the secret of the only true liberty there is—a freedom that gladly accepts fetters:

> Make me a captive, Lord,
> And then I shall be free.

Prayer and a
Poultice

A YOUNG minister's preacher-father was on his death bed. Following a fall he had been unconscious for days. From the anxious hearts of the family fervent prayers arose without ceasing. The dear one now hovering between life and death had been the glad bearer of glad tidings for more than a half-century. For years he had been the loved pastor of the same church in the national capital. In zeal and love abounding, his life had been lived under spires of the spirit. Now, in his retirement, this accident had happened. The very best in modern medical skill was focused on that room where this faithful servant of the Most High lay. Prayer and medicine were joined as, day after day, the final verdict hung in the balance.

The son was keeping watch in the hospital room where his father lay. The crisis might come at any time. It was uncertain when the younger man could again stand in his own pulpit of a large church in a southern city; his place then was by his mother's side as together they kept a vigil of hope and love. But in those still hours, as the clock ticked the days away, the young proclaimer of the Eternal Word, with pad on his knee, was writing a message to be delivered whenever he could face once again the sympathetic flock of his busy parish. It happened that the sermon written in that quiet hospital room was not preached until after the father had slipped through death's door into a larger room of the Father's many-mansioned house.

What was it that the son decided to preach about as he pondered and wrote with his father's unconscious form so close to where he sat? The most effective preaching is so often colored by impinging circumstances. How often, when he ascends the pulpit stairs, the message in the preacher's heart mirrors his own experiences and inner life or those of the ones who look to him for the bread of life! This was so often true of the "preaching" of that One who spoke as no one had ever spoken before—or has since.

In this instance, the frame for the sermon was the Old Testament story of the good ruler Hezekiah, king of Judah, who was at the point of death. By the sick king's side was the prophet Isaiah. Some sort of infection threatened the life of the righteous young king. It is recorded that, faced by death, he turned his tearful countenance to the wall and poured out his heart to God in a torrent of beseeching prayer. That prayer of faith was a factor in healing the sick. Hezekiah had many years added to his life.

Now let us give you the text for this sickroom sermon: "Hezekiah . . . prayed to the LORD. . . . And Isaiah said, 'Bring a cake of figs. And let them take and lay it on the boil, that he may recover.'" Here is the magic combination staring at us out of the centuries long, long ago—prayer and a poultice.

(The remainder of this spire was written by the one who bears his father's full name, Andrew R. Bird.)

Two things were responsible for Hezekiah's recovery—prayer and a poultice, or faith and works. Without either of these techniques Hezekiah might have died in the prime of life. One lesson that lies on the face of this story is that although prayer is essential, it must never be made a substitute for human skill and effort. Faith without works is dead. Isaiah was a man of great piety, but he was also a sensible man and did not neglect the poultice. We must pray as if everything depended upon God, and then work as if everything depended upon us.

There are those who make the mistake of thinking that they have to choose between prayer and a poultice—between faith and medicine. There are those who, under the spell of a strange piety, scorn the marvels of medical science. Witness the healing cults with their fantastic reasoning—as if God were not the giver of every good and perfect gift. And there are others who, with human pride, disdain the power of believing and persistent prayer—as suggested by the practical paganism of some modern doctors.

A new day for the healing of men's bodies seems to be dawning as the representatives of religion, psychiatry, and medicine pool their resources and work together in mutual confidence and practical helpfulness. Prayer and a poultice belong together, and it is both stupid and shameful to neglect the benefits of either.

It is not prayer or a poultice; it is not faith or medicine. It is not either/or, but both/and. "The full truth," wrote the great theologian Karl Barth, "flies like a bird with two wings; and maimed in either by our partial thinking it flutters a crippled creature on the ground."

This is God's plan, in the Old Testament and the New, to show us that in all of life faith and works are partners. The formula is prayer and a poultice. Faith and works belong together. Are yours together?

When Evil Is
Good

PERHAPS the greatest fallacy of this generation is the belief that the chief aim of life is to make it as easy as possible—as the old hymn put it, "to be carried to the skies on flowery beds of ease." Of course, it is cause for great gratitude that the discoveries in the medical field have cleared life's way of so many once-dreaded diseases. It is a boon, indeed, that certain drugs relieve the body of excruciating pain for which there was once no release except death. It is a cause for constant Te Deums that the dreary burden of strength-sapping toil has been so largely taken over by ingenious machines which operate at the touch of a button.

However, we are too close to the struggle of primitive days not to be constantly reminded of the dividends that come both to the body and to the character through the challenge of self-denial, of personal initiative, and of battling with frowning difficulties. With a hundred mechanized slaves working for every one of us in this decade, it is still inspiring to look at the seamed face of Abraham Lincoln and recall the formative surroundings of his early career in the University of Hard Knocks.

It was thirty-five years after that great captain of his time came to the tragic end of his career, so buffeted by evil and hardship and disappointment, that John Ruskin, the great Englishman, died. A brilliant editorial on his contribution to literature reads, "His own life was a sequence of tragedies, many of them bitter and cruel, yet without such successive ordeals of frustration, Ruskin might have been a total failure in his work."

That appraisal of the role of hardship in one life can be authenticated in a thousand biographies as men and women have fared forth to meet their date with destiny.

A famous naturalist related how, in pity, he watched the struggle of a chrysalis to break out of a cocoon. Following his impulse to help, he took his knife and cut the silken casket to make the process easier. But what emerged was a weak creature with anemic body and bleached wings, unable to fly. This is a kind of parable showing that there are times when evil is good, as estimated in the final outcome.

Without what at the time seems evil we humans might be secure yet morally spineless automatons. History records that it is not the people in the lotus lands of the tropics, lying back lazily in the balmy air under waving palm trees, who are strong and adventurous; rather, it is those where the climate and the elements make a constant struggle inevitable who are the builders of great civilizations.

Our old boyhood favorite, *Robinson Crusoe,* if read between the lines—or even on the lines—unfolds a story in which what was labeled evil turns out to be good. The pagan savage, Friday, asked our early hero of the lonely island a pertinent question. Crusoe had told the savage about a loving God who was all-powerful. He explained the evil in the world by blaming Satan for all that was bad. The puzzled man, Friday, came back with the question, "Then why God no kill the devil?" That query humiliated and puzzled his teacher. He had no valid answer, but later, as more chapters were written in the book of experience, he saw at least a glimmering of an explanation of the embarrassing dilemma raised by his devoted servant.

Said the stranded Crusoe, "I began to be very well contented with the life that I was leading if only I could have been secure from the dread of savages." But finally, when he came to count the wealth that had flowed into his life from the day when he first saw the footprints on the sand, he confessed, "Very frequently the evil which we seek most to shun, and which is the most dread to us, is the very means and door of our deliverance."

The story is told of a fisherman who seemed to have a secret unknown to any of the others with regard to his fish. Every fishmonger knew that the fish from the tank of this one boat of the fleet would be as fine and firm and vigorous as if they had just been dumped there from a net. The fish of the other fishermen, although alive, were soft and flabby and listless. In vain his comrades tried to unravel the mystery, but through the years he was as silent as the sphinx.

After his death his daughter carried out her father's instructions and told the secret. It was simply that he kept a pugnacious catfish or two in the well of his boat. These fighting fish kept the other fish in a state of alert agitation and alarm. Compelled to live thus always with vigilance similar to their normal life in the sea, they maintained their stamina and strength. The utter security of all the other tanks resulted in the deterioration of the favored fish.

And so, to ask the question, "Why God no kill the devil?" or "Why did not the old fisherman kill the catfish?" is to suggest that evil has its uses. Maltbie Babcock knew that truth as far as human life is concerned when he wrote, "Be strong! ... Shun not the struggle: face it, 'tis God's gift."

In the Louvre there is a picture by Guido Reni of Michael with his foot on Satan's neck. William James, with keen insight, expressed the richness of its allegorical meaning in one sentence: "The world is all the richer for having a devil in it so long as we keep our foot upon his neck."

Roses in the Heart

Hosts of Americans with eyes to see and hearts to feel would gratefully agree that an effulgent part of the deluge of June's loveliness is roses. But of course arbors of roses are cherished around the earth. When Rudyard Kipling wrote "Our England Is a Garden," part of his inspiration came from quaint thatched cottages framed with rose-covered porches. George Washington's forebears came from that gardened island and brought the garden passion to the New World, making the wilderness blossom like the rose.

When the longest day of the year is past and spring gives way to summer, we go on into the sultry time of harvests with a floral doxology for the still abundant roses. What artist with speech or canvas can paint the ravishing glory of roses red and white, pink and yellow?

Two friends are pictured peering through a train window at the changing rural panorama. That is one of the gilt-edged dividends of a train ride in contrast to travel by plane. These friends found themselves looking at a sun-drenched meadow in which perhaps fifty cows were peacefully grazing, feeding as one. Looking through that picture window, one of the two spoke of the lucrative livestock industry that the cattle suggested. But with apparently little interest in beef for the tables of the nation, or even milk for its dairies, the other eagerly exclaimed, "Just look at those lovely daisies!" Then, pointing to a huge patch of them in a corner of the sunny meadow, he remarked frankly, "There is more hope for humanity in a wild flower than in tons of beef."

Later, the first man found himself wondering just what had been meant by his companion, whose eyes were more fascinated by a cowslip than by a cow! Turning it over in his mind, he realized that his daisy-minded friend was not minimizing the importance of food for the table but was simply trying to say that any flower is one of life's extras—one of those things that we do not have to have but which we cherish all the more for that very reason.

Dwelling thus on this world of flowers, the first man stumbled upon a conception that has colored all his future thinking. He expressed it in these words: "Life supplies us with only two kinds of things, necessities and extras. Some like air, water, food, shelter—these are among the bare necessities—with them we can exist. But moonlight and starlight, dawnings and sunsets, flowers and music, are distinctly extras." And then he added this confession: "A thoughtful consideration of life's extras has done more to give my faith in God actual conviction than all the sermons I ever heard." And surely one of God's great extras is the rose!

Some time ago, after I had been in the midst of a rather prosaic task for hours, I glanced out the window and beheld two gorgeous redbirds together on a leafy branch. Instantly that pair of cardinals wrote for me an IOU for extras.

Who on shipboard has not turned from the garish trivialities of the gilded salon to the heaving deck, there to revel in the sacrament of beauty as a jeweled pathway of dazzling splendor was flung by the high-riding moon across the vastness of the deep?

In a volume entitled *God's Extras,* the dean of an English cathedral wrote a chapter called "Roses." When a preacher friend of mine read it, he said, "The very first sentence in the book is well worth the money I gave for it. Ever since I opened the volume for the first time that golden sentence has been singing itself over and over in my brain. Here it is: 'He who would have beautiful roses in his garden must have beautiful roses in his heart.' "

One of the most queenly women it was ever my privilege to know, whose life seemed full of many-tinted lovelinesses and the silky petals of the beauty of holiness, and who passionately loved roses, used to say again and again, "You have to cultivate roses on your knees."

Roses in the heart—what a fragrant phrase that is! There is One whose heart is so full of roses that he was, himself, called "The Rose." Following him will tell us how to turn the wilderness of our hearts into gardens of sweetly scented roses.

It could be said of the life of George Matheson, who reveled in God's extras, that he had beautiful roses in his heart. As the darkness of blindness was closing in upon him, this lover of roses wrote a hymn that has upon it the breath of immortality. It is about that One who was called "The Rose of Sharon." Out of his own poignant experience, when so much seemed to be snatched from his life, Matheson penned the words, "O Love that wilt not let me go." At his funeral the students of Edinburgh carried a mammoth wreath of his favorite flowers. The grave was piled high with red roses.

Knowing that Matheson always had beautiful roses in his garden and beautiful roses in his heart, one can see those red blossoms waving triumphantly in that gem of hymnology he wrote:

> I lay in dust life's glory dead,
> And from the ground there
>   blossoms red
> Life that shall endless be.

Unused
Goodness

Nothing concerns Americans more than the tragic contrast between our stored-up food and the empty stomachs of most of the world. Unused grain, costing a million dollars a day just to store, does not make sense in the hungry world. But into that perplexing problem with all its moral and economic and cold-war overtones we cannot go, except to say that food means survival and that daily bread for all peoples is the most potent factor in making a peaceful world. There is no more damning indictment of the Communist system than that, in spite of all its rosy promises, it cannot adequately feed its deluded people, who are taught to hate a system whose fruitage is food to spare.

Although unused food is a most challenging problem, there is an even greater question suggested by every place of divine worship whatever its name or sign. Churches and synagogues are symbols of righteousness, of moral integrity, of goodness. The question raised by every skyward spire has to do with unused goodness. While from our hearts we say, with Abraham

Lincoln, "thanks be unto God who in our great trial giveth us the churches," we are also forced to confess, unfortunately, that the churches are often spiritual granaries where so much unused goodness is stored.

Bliss Carman was thinking of the unused goodness to be found in churches when he assured rampant evil it had little to fear from much that went on one day in seven behind stained-glass windows:

> They're praising God on Sunday,
> They'll be all right on Monday.
> It's just a little habit they've acquired!

Such a statement poses for everyone whose passionate objective is to possess genuine goodness the pertinent question, "What are you doing with the goodness you profess?" The one effective antidote for the rampant evil of today is goodness that is really used.

The chief hindrance to the progress of the race toward golden and shining goals is not the violently bad, but the passively good. Against such people no just charges of venal culpability can be raised. They are not viciously bad, but neither are they aggressively good. The insidious temptation of even the prodigiously pious is to be good—for nothing. Those who yield to this temptation have been labeled "the vacillating, inconsistent good."

One of the greatest stories ever told is the narrative about the Good Samaritan. But did you ever notice that the matchless narrator uttered no tirade about the lack of police protection along the robber-infested Jericho Road? He made no arraignment of the criminal who waylaid and wounded the traveler. What he did was to point to two good men who, witnessing dire need, callously passed by on the other side. The parable might well be called "the sin of unused goodness."

That etching suggests church members content with just being respectable. Oh yes, they are good! They have enough religion to be decent but not enough to be dynamic. They have some faith—enough to make them recoil from the grosser forms of sin but not enough to make them spiritual crusaders.

117

It was the realization of how much goodness is stored, instead of being poured, that led Maltbie Babcock to pen the verse in his hymn with the ringing exhortation:

> Be strong! Say not the days
>   are evil—who's to blame?
> And fold the hands and
>   acquiesce—O shame!
> Stand up, speak out, and
>   bravely, in God's Name,
> Be strong, be strong!

That good minister, when he wrote those lines, had in his heart the thrill of the early church in which there was an oppressive sense of a desperate conflict, a fight to the death with malignant and powerful evil. The church of the New Testament never thought of itself as being in a rest camp: it was obviously on a battle line.

An inspiring religious leader of our day, thinking of unused goodness, declared:

The weakness of some parts of the church today is the loss of that positive quality of its life. It lies in the fact that many people who ought to be struggling against social wrongs are not so much fighters as like dear old ladies in snowy white caps sitting in rocking chairs, not really knowing that any fight is going on.

The Communists know there is! The good people of America had better!

Too many have been brought up to think that goodness means repression; but goodness consists in living for those things which alone are worth living for. That vision often is not shared by those who are only negatively good.

A rather bored wife wrote to one whose column is a repository of worried people's peeves and problems. She said she had been married for many years to a man who did not swear, or drink, or smoke, or gamble, or carouse. But she had become fed up with his impeccable goodness, a piety that was not harnessed to anything worthwhile and consisted only of things that he did not do. Judging from her complaint, her life companion did not know the meaning of righteous indignation.

Who has not encountered this brand of humanity whose motto is, "I am better than thou," whose main drive in life is "safety first," and whose favorite seat in any contest is the fence? When a fight is on, and the call is to stand up and be counted, such folks want to take their goodness up to a reserved seat in the balcony. They seem to choose the permanent role of being an inquiring neutral. That attitude has been diagnosed as "spectatoritis." Whatever virtues they have must be labeled "Unused Goodness."

A Book and a Nook

WITH all their frantic journeyings and searching for new scenes, there is in most summer seekers the yearning for quiet nooks. One is not likely to be in a vacation oasis very long before crowds begin to pall, glittering attractions dim, the mania for that which is new subsides, and one looks for some inspiration point where he can be alone. The vista from such a spot may be the sea, a lake, a garden, a smiling landscape, a leafy grove, or any number of other appealing outlooks.

As a companion for such quiet hours when, with the busy world shut out, we invite our souls, I recommend a book so small that it can be carried in any pocket or handbag with no obtrusive bulge. Yet, it is the most amazing packet of spiritual vitamins for inner therapy the ages have discovered. The man who put down these spiritual prescriptions died a score of years before America was discovered. His name—Thomas a Kempis.

About the only verbal candid shot of him we have is that he was a diminutive man who spent his life in a monastery. He was "fresh-colored" and as he came from his cell for devotions, he stood upright as if on tiptoe when the Psalms were chanted. Added to that faded picture is the comment of a companion about this medieval monk to the effect that he liked best of all "little books and quiet nooks."

It was a time when thrones were tottering and social turmoil was high. The noisy clatter of change was heard in the air.

But in the midst of it this one individual managed to live his patient life of introspection and contemplation and to cast into pearl-like sentences thoughts that will be treasured as long as the race endures. Thomas a Kempis little knew that he was writing the biggest little book of all the centuries and constructing for multitudes who would come after him a glorious arbor that no one whose greatest inner need is a quiet nook can afford not to find.

And so, a golden piece of advice in this day, when routine duties are often overwhelming, is—find a nook at home or away, it does not matter, and commune with this book. It will leap heavenward like a pointing spire! It is no exaggeration to call it perhaps the tallest spire any one man has ever reared.

In her day George Eliot declared, as she spoke of the miracles performed by this small old-fashioned volume, that it turns "bitter waters into sweetness." It became her lifelong companion and was on her pillow when she died.

When Nurse Edith Cavell languished in a wretched prison at Brussels, awaiting execution, she cherished as her greatest treasure and solace her copy of this blessed little book, which came out of the cells and cloisters of centuries past. In her last moments she begged that when it was all over her copy of *The Imitation* be sent to a beloved cousin in England.

The little book I am recommending as a vacation companion is, with the exception of the Holy Bible, the most amazing volume in the world. Although it was written five centuries ago, Catholics and Protestants alike unite in acknowledging that they owe infinite things to its elixir. It simply refuses to repose on the high shelves of oblivion. Even in this age when there is no end to the number of books being published, this volume has gone into six thousand editions and has been translated into more than fifty languages.

There are cures offered in up-to-date psychological kits for all the discords that spoil the music of life, but the best antidote for these disturbing notes is not to be found in any twentieth-century wonder drug guaranteeing attainment of peace and poise. The most effective directions for escaping from "the little foxes, that spoil the vineyards" are not to be found in any Book of the Month. They are lifted up in the Book of the Centuries and its title is *The Imitation of Christ*. This titanic little classic has in it the stored power to redeem this fear-haunted world, cleansing individual hearts as well as social and international relations, if it is but heard and heeded.

Surely no man in our times lived more in our world, and yet was not of it, than Rufus Jones, the great Quaker. There are no hours of greater spiritual exaltation than those spent in a nook somewhere with anything written by Rufus Jones in one's hands. In the introduction to my own worn copy of *The Imitation* (treasured above rubies), he has this to say:

This book has worked miracles in every generation since it was written. It has helped untold thousands to turn defeat to victory and despair to optimism. This poor monk's vision of eternal reality makes the soul forget its temporal miseries. It will continue to attract as long as the heart pants for the living God!

In your retreat to some quiet nook with this book, first of all write on the flyleaf George Herbert's words: "By all means use some time to be alone. Salute thyself. See what thy soul doth wear." And then, add this sentence from *The Imitation* itself:

"Blessed are those who are glad to have time to spare for God!"

The Need for Uncommon
Common Men

THE LATE President Kennedy, speaking at Amherst College, declared that "personal distinction" is a "must" if the United States is to survive as a strong and free nation. America was founded by men of personal distinction!

At another college, Lafayette, in addressing a graduating class, Thomas J. Watson, of IBM, declared: "The world's destiny will, to a great extent, depend on how many 'uncommon' men and women we have. If we fail to produce them in sufficient numbers we will fail as a nation." These assertions are based upon the certainty which history gives us that the future of the so-called common man is always in the hands of the "uncommon" man.

In spite of the fact that there is an aristocracy of brains and energy, one of the dire dangers of democracy is the worship of the average. Excellence is often something to be disdained and ridiculed. In politics one who excels in ability and knowledge is often disparagingly called an "egghead." In education one who pays the price for scholarship, and so is rated far above the average, is called a "grind" or a "square." But the curse of democracy is conformity to the lowest common denominator. The real rule of the people involves not a leveling down but a lifting up. The hope of the race's future is always in those gifted to push ahead of the crowd.

Former President Herbert Hoover, out of his ripe sagacity, left us this warning:

We are in danger of developing a cult of the common man, which means a cult of mediocrity. Let us remember that the great human advances have not been brought about by mediocre men and women. We believe in equal opportunity for all but we know that this includes the opportunity to rise to leadership—in other words, to be "uncommon." To be realistic we must agree that in a profound sense men and women are not equal. Certainly not in practical ability. It would be contrary to history and to observable facts to declare that all men, if given the same chance, are equal in intellectual capacity.

There was once a family of nine children in New England, all with the same home training, but in it was only one Daniel Webster. There is no way to explain that enigma. As someone put it: "Some men put the pressure on their brains and find them alert, eager, and competent, and others turn on the current of their intellectual ambitions with no better consequence than blowing out a fuse."

This is a time to realize that the strength of democracy depends not just on the right to vote but on informed and intelligent voters. Blind loyalty to a cash register type of democracy is deadening! One comes to realize that there are instances when two and two do not make four. Sometimes it seems that even our courts and our legislative bodies are not sufficiently aware of that.

A lawyer was reeling off mountains of mathematical computations, but the judge thought he was trying to make them mean more than they did. It was like the pricking of a balloon which hot legal breath had vastly inflated, when the judge quietly interpolated, "But two and two, you know, do not always make four. You could scarcely say that two candles plus two tons of coal make four."

The weakness of democracy as often interpreted is that it gives the ignoramus, the lawbreaker, the moral leper, and the scoundrel the same voice in the affairs of state as a man of intelligence and integrity to whom the whole community looks up with respect. It is this assumption that the acme of democracy is simply to make sure that all noses are counted, that led George Gissing to make one of his characters blurt out: "I hate the very word 'majority.' It is the few, the very few, that have always kept alive whatever good we see in the race."

Christianity never tries to evade the fact of individual differences. It assumes in any society the presence of the strong and the weak. Alas, it is covetousness of the gifts of others that eats like a cancer and spoils life's sweetest music. The fruits of the most highly endowed are all ours, and the eyes of the common man, no matter how close to the common ground, are free to feast on the highest and the best that the race knows.

It was to a pretty average company of believers that Paul wrote, "All things are yours." And so, looking starward from the murky mediocrity with which perhaps we touch elbows, we listen to that further injunction of the great apostle: ". . . if there is any excellence, if there is anything worthy of praise, think about these things." To every one of us belongs the excellence of the uncommon common man.

When Saul Eyed David

"SAUL EYED DAVID." Thus in three master strokes the Scriptures give us this vivid verbal etching. Saul's heart was gripped with envy because of the popularity captured by David in his dramatic victory over Goliath. The dancing women were chanting the praise of the shepherd boy instead of extolling the king. It was in a passion of envy that Saul hurled a javelin at his youthful competitor for the people's admiration and affection. It is not a pretty picture, but it has been reproduced countless times across the ages.

In the tangled tale of human behavior, no motive is more dangerously potent than envy. It is the impish culprit that pulls the strings for much of the unworthy acting on life's varied stage. If one yields to its malignant temptation, at last it eats like a canker and destroys the finest elements of character. To conquer envy is to be on the way to moral grandeur.

Goethe had a piercing insight that led him to declare, "Against the great superiority of others there is no remedy but love." Jealousy turns the one who allows it houseroom into a slave. Envy is the explanation of more slander, half-truths, and discounting gossip on the lips of individuals than any other emotion that poisons human relationships.

A good friend of mine wrote this sentence: "He who is conscious that envy has found lodgment in his soul, who knows of someone whose success creates an emotion of resentment and covetousness in his heart and calls forth expressions of depreciation and criticism should closely examine himself and cast himself humbly on the mercy of God."

In any list of the deadliest sins, envy, of necessity, is included.

At the Washington Cathedral there is a group of sculptured figures representing, in modern dress, the top seven vices in the aristocracy of evil. Here in contemporary clothes are those perennial foes of saintliness which have worn the prevailing fashions of every age, under all skies. They seem like gargoyles endeavoring to preach a sermon in stone as they surround the central figure of Penance. Envy appropriately is symbolized by a figure dressed in dismal garb, lacking money to buy the luxuries of life but ogling enviously the fur coat of a wealthy man.

Dr. Fosdick held up a mirror to our common humanity when he keenly remarked:

How many folks there are who can live kindly with inferiors and amicably with equals, but who grow hard and envious as soon as they deal with folks who surpass them! We compete with a rival, and are beaten, and something as old as Cain wakes up in us and gives us a tussle before we are done with it.

Ah, yes, we all know it and might as well confess it. One of the most difficult of spiritual exercises is to praise the very excellence by which we are surpassed.

One of the saintliest of men, Andrew Bonar, wrote in his diary twenty years after he entered the ministry: "Envy is my hurt. And today I have been seeking grace to rejoice exceedingly over the usefulness of others even when it casts me into the shade."

That sin, whose blight John the Baptist escaped as he said of the Master, "He must increase, but I must decrease," nevertheless pushed its way even into the circle closest to the great Galilean who was the servant of all. For even as the disciples sat at the table with the matchless Nazarene, as the black circle of treachery was closing in upon him, "a dispute also arose among them, which of them was to be regarded as the greatest."

Ill feeling between nations is fed by envy of the power or privilege of other people. It poisons even the united front of allies who face a common foe. The bitterness of so-called class divisions does not always grow out of want. Often the most envious have plenty. Their trouble is jealousy!

Who doubts that envy is the master passion of the ruthless policy of expansion? It is that which makes the Communists announce ludicrous and unfounded claims about the priority of their alleged inventions. The Iron Curtain largely is to shut out the enticing sights that would make the depressed population envious of what it is told is the effete West.

No wonder that under *covet* the dictionary says "See *envy*." For covetousness is the poisonous fruit springing from that evil seed. The road to the Utopia of which all nations dream is paved with the material of humility and sharing of a love that rejoices in another's success.

In the apostolic exhortation, "Let us have no self-conceit, no provoking of one another, no envy of one another," Paul knew full well that the covetous eye always is closely linked with the hurled javelin of envy!

The Curtain of
Light

Amid today's human convulsions shaking the planet, national curtains are quite the fashion. Just as the confident assertion was being made, in a world whose nations were fast becoming one, that the day of artificial fences was a thing of the past, lo, the thickest walls ever known were being thrown around millions to isolate them from other millions. The one system which loudly advertises to the workers of the world that it proposes to tear down all partitions between groups and whose avowed goal is a classless society, attempts to erect, surrounding its far borders, a curtain so opaque that it is called iron. This is to prevent the light that is on the outside from dispelling the darkness that is on the inside.

We hear much also about the so-called bamboo curtain flung around the vast reaches of China. A well-known newspaperman who escaped to tell the world in an uncensored broadcast what is really taking place in China drew this picture: "Everything is being dragooned into the party pattern. The newspapers publish only what is acceptable to Peking, while every effort is made, for instance, by the exclusion of foreign news agencies, to cut the Chinese people off from knowledge of what is happening abroad." The idea is to keep regimented slaves back of spike fences, in ignorance of the world outside their borders, and to feed them false impressions of the past history and the present position of their own country in its relation to the rest of the world.

H. G. Wells wrote a short story with the title "The Country of the Blind." In it he described a race of people, in an inaccessible valley, who had lost their sight. When, by accident, a traveler reached their valley and told them of a world in which there is light and color and spoke to them of the rising and the setting sun, of the sky at night covered with stars, they believed that he was mad or the victim of some mysterious disease. Their world of darkness was to them the real world—the only world they knew—and they could imagine nothing outside it or better than it. That is a parable of what happens to people who live in an inaccessible world back of curtains. Those who put up such partitions watch with cruel eyes lest there should leak through from the outside world information that might refute the official propaganda.

But there is still another curtain which may be thrown not around the children of darkness, but around the children of light. Even we of the West, or the East, who scoff at curtains whose strands are fashioned of fear and inferiority complexes, may unconsciously use the very light in which we revel as a curtain that hides from view the tragic facts of others less privileged than we. The old expression "I was blinded by the light" may have implications to which we need to be alerted.

In depicting the Florence of Savonarola in her monumental novel *Romola*, George Eliot coined a phrase that opens up warning vistas regarding this matter of curtains. She said, "The light can be a curtain, as well as the darkness." Ah, here is a danger of which we, in privileged America, need to be made vividly aware, lest we construct a curtain even out of our light!

When people are dazzled by effulgence, their eyes cease to function. A curtain of light makes them oblivious to that which is around them. They are blinded. Perhaps it would not torture the meaning of a striking saying of the Great Galilean to quote it as a warning against using light as a curtain: "If then the light in you is darkness, how great is the darkness!" Privilege has a sly way of concealing from the pampered how the other half lives, whether across the railroad tracks or across the world. Light may blind as well as reveal.

In the days of the Russian czars, around the brilliant court surfeited with luxuries, a curtain of light hid from the ruling class the plight of the exploited populace.

A well-known remark is attributed to a French queen who was also isolated by a royal curtain of light. When one dared to tell her that her subjects had no bread, she replied, "Let them eat cake."

The New Testament tells of the pride-smitten Pharisee who, because of his own luminous halo, could not see that in the despised publican beside him were qualities that heaven appraised as golden, while his own alleged virtues were seen as what they were—worthless glitter.

A survey in New York, city of the Great White Way, revealed that in that vast metropolitan center there were a quarter of a million bedrooms into which no direct breath of air or ray of sunshine has ever come since they were built. Living in comfort in that same city, a great Christian leader expressed deep concern because so many of God's children were forced to exist in such dark caverns. "But," said a friend, "you ought not to blame yourself for that."

"No," said this outstanding citizen, "but it is of prime importance that I should recognize it and that I should say to myself, 'You have been privileged, and so probably you are socially blind—blind as an owl at noonday—to what is going on in society and what ultimately ought to go on.' "

In an exciting political campaign Gladstone declared that a curtain of privilege during the preceding half-century had so blinded the possessing classes that they had been on the wrong side of every great social issue. There is no greater danger, as far as the world of tomorrow is concerned, than that this nation, the most opulent history has ever known, living in a million-watt illumination amid its shining mechanical gadgets catering to comfort, pleasure, and convenience, should be so blinded by the glare about it as to miss the significance of the revolution sweeping the world today, especially in Asia, demanding more abundant life for the teeming hosts of that half of the earth existing in misery and hunger.

God bless America with power to see beyond its curtain of light, lest some future historian refer to her in a footnote to the "Tale of the Twentieth Century" as "the country of the blind." God bless America with wisdom to see that light, as well as darkness, may be a curtain.

On Playing
Second Fiddle

PLAYING second fiddle long has been the synonym of failure to reach the summit in any line of endeavor. It is regarded as the epitaph of a frustrated ambition. How often the suggestion that one be content with what some might label a secondary role is met by the petulant, indignant rejoinder, "I won't play second fiddle to anybody." Such a refusal often is a telltale revelation that one who cares more for recognition than contribution is not really fit to play either first fiddle or second in the orchestra of life.

The youth of this competitive day are often spurred on by what has been called the drum-major complex. They have been taught to be keenly aware of outlets for display. As has been aptly said, "We all want to play Hamlet." Success means the head of the parade where, with whirling baton, the exhibitionist instinct can run, have free course, and be glorified. Life is regarded as a ruthless race and, in spite of polished and polite amenities, the goal is to outstrip all competitors and, crowned with laurel, to be acclaimed as victor. But, alas, this road ends in dust and ashes.

The truth is that the apex is not the whole of the pyramid. Ninety-nine percent is the sustaining base beneath the highest point. There would be no isolated height were it not for the dependable foundation that holds it up. An orchestra is not all first fiddles. The proportion of those who reach that distinction is small compared to the proportion who make their contributions on other instruments to the total effect of the swelling music.

The caliber of a performer is indicated not by the place he occupies or the instrument he plays, but by the quality of work rendered in the niche that is his. A poor second fiddle can spoil the music of a whole orchestra. As a matter of fact, the most insignificant work of the world always has been committed to the hands of those who would be appraised by their contemporaries as second fiddlers. But that is the most honorable fraternity of the centuries. It also offers the most durable satisfactions. Fame is notoriously unhappy. Uneasy is the head that wears any crown. The limelight of distinction makes one the target for carping criticism. So-called celebrities envy those whose cup of joy is full as, away from the scorching searchlight of public attention, they play "second fiddle." Life's most vital lesson is that in all fields it is not what you play, but how you play, that greatly matters.

In his *Random Reminiscences,* the actor Charles Brookfield, who always was assigned minor roles on the stage, tells of a rather startling and revealing incident in his career. He was very ill with an acute attack of pleurisy. In some way the rumor started that the disease had proved fatal. The evening papers carried the news with his obituary. There were the usual gracious things that are said when death has come. Propped up in bed, the alleged dead man read the eulogies pronounced on himself. One paper declared, "Though Mr. Brookfield was never a great actor, he was invaluable in small parts." Think of reading that about oneself! It really said he was a splendid second fiddler. The actor thought a finer compliment could not have been paid him.

In the total sum of the things most worthwhile the highest tribute goes to those who are invaluable in small parts. Marconi, of wireless fame, paid a heartfelt tribute to one whose help forty years before had led to his own great discoveries. "Without that man," he testified, "my work would have been impossible." One who in any realm is lifted to some shining pinnacle of recognition, applauded, canonized, and admired, knows in his heart that he is there because he stands on some more obscure man's shoulders. What a golden volume could be written entitled *Tributes to Those Who Have Played Second Fiddle!*

The ultimate strength of any institution lies in the unspectacular and out-of-sight people whom expert appraisers, with their secular registers, would likely put in the category of second fiddlers. Well has it been said: "Maturity attests itself as a person becomes content to play a humble part in life's orchestra, concerned only that the symphony be played and the composer fittingly interpreted."

Once, while rehearsing Beethoven's Ninth Symphony, Toscanini, who had led the orchestra with a fire in his soul which touched each player, after the thrilling finale said softly to the enthralled musicians: "Why am I? Who is Toscanini? I am nobody. Who are you? You are nobody. I am nobody and you are nobody." And then with arms extended and face glowing, he whispered: "It's Beethoven. He is everything." It was enough that every instrument and every player had helped to show forth the glory which the composer saw and felt. What mattered the musical instrument any one of the performers played? It was the passion for perfection that had welded the separate artists into an inspiring musical unity.

Once, to the Master of Life who was concerned with nothing except the Oratorio of Redemption came an anxious mother, pleading that her two boys be given the position of playing first fiddle. That very ambition showed that she and they had missed the point and the way.

In perhaps the most sacred scene in the entire New Testament gallery of masterpieces, one with eyes to see could not miss an uplifted sign: Wanted—A Servant to Wash Feet! But not one of the group volunteered for that necessary, menial task. No one would play second fiddle. Then comes a sentence in the record that is astounding in its implications: "Jesus, knowing that . . . he had come from God and was going to God, . . . girded himself with a towel. Then he poured water into a basin, and began to wash the disciples' feet." He himself became the servant as he stooped to conquer.

With awe, one has written under that picture, "Infinite power with a towel on its arm!" Wonder of wonders!

A modern humble follower of that great Nazarene, the famed preacher Charles A. Spurgeon, gratefully traced the beginning of his own great career to a snowy Sunday morning when, as a boy, with only a handful at church, he heard an unknown lay preacher, a second fiddler, who gripped and won him. Long afterward, that renowned pulpiteer pointed to an Alpine peak of truth in two lines:

> It needs more skill than I can tell
> To play the second fiddle well.

A Glorious Gift to
Liberty

SOME time ago the storied rotunda of the United States Capitol was crowded by grateful patriots from all parts of the Republic. The outstanding occasion was the dedication of the sculptured countenance of Constantino Brumidi, from whose artistic hands the Capitol walls will always speak.

Many years ago, an Italian immigrant, forty-seven years of age, came to the United States. For him freedom beckoned in this blessed land of room enough. For years he had steeped himself in the mural glories of the Vatican and had helped to restore the faded Raphael frescoes.

With that background he yearned, somehow with his art, to express his growing gratitude for the vast benefits he found waiting in his adopted land. Once in America, his gifted brush and soaring imagination were dedicated to sacred subjects. Shortly after, he was given his great chance when he was commissioned to embellish the expanding Capitol of the United States. This opportunity thrilled him.

Millions of pilgrims from all parts of the nation and the globe now gaze with admiration at the speaking walls on which Constantino Brumidi breathed the haunting beauty that burned in his poetic soul. As he kept working patiently through the years, out of his artistic cornucopia came varied forms and figures clinging to the walls and ceilings in gorgeous colors and rich designs.

Wherever Brumidi toiled in the vast Capitol, the walls began to speak. In spite of detracting criticism and a lack of appreciation, he kept patiently at his task for almost a quarter of a century. The walls of the historic Capitol were his offering to the God of liberty and beauty, and his genius was a golden gift.

Perhaps the climax of all his Capitol treasures is what is known as the "President's Room" on the Senate side. For more than six years he toiled on that jeweled ceiling. The bequest he left there has given it the distinction of being called the most exquisitely decorated room in America.

The Capitol rotunda contains his magnificent frieze of fifteen historical groupings, capped by his huge frescoed canopy in the eye of the Capitol dome, measuring 4,664 square feet of concave fresco. His work flourished until a tragic fall, while he was working on the rotunda frieze, terminated his labors.

Less than a week after his death a prophecy was uttered on the floor of the United States Senate: "One day Brumidi will be crowned by the gratitude of succeeding generations." However, republics are notoriously ungrateful. It seems to be an unfortunate trait of democracy that often its most shining servants and saints are those who are cannonaded while alive and canonized only long after death has removed them beyond the reach of praise or blame.

From his commissioning in 1855 to his death, Brumidi's work on the Capitol was his passion. As he put it, "I no longer have any desire for fame or fortune. My one ambition, and my daily prayer, is that I may live long enough to make beautiful the Capitol of the one country in the world in which there is liberty."

Brumidi died in 1880 and was buried in an unmarked grave in Washington's Glenwood Cemetery. It took seventy-two years in the history of a forgetful nation before a persistent woman finally pleaded to Congress to authorize a bronze marker for the grave of this Patriot of the Brush, who embellished those hallowed walls! It was that same elect lady, Dr. Myrtle Cheney Murdock, her heart shamed at such flagrant ingratitude, who published in 1950 an illustrated volume, an exquisite example of the bookmaker's art, reproducing in glorious color the immortal frescoes for all America to see and admire. It is entitled *Constantino Brumidi, Michelangelo of the United States Capitol.*

It was indeed fitting that the highest officials of the United States Congress asked this splendid lady, who did so much for the Capitol, to unveil the Brumidi bust in the "Westminster Abbey" of our national remembrance. In the historic beauty of those speaking walls Brumidi, though dead, still lives!

America's
Amen

"Amen" is the diamond among the gems of devotion. It is a hallowed word hedged about with sanctity. It is the sign of a vow registered in heaven. It is both supplication and affirmation.

The Book of books is like a vast cathedral in which through the long centuries there has resounded again and again the sound of a great "amen." From age to age the sacred writings have been punctuated with such expressions as "and all the people shall answer and say, 'Amen.'"

When the law was read to the vast assemblage, first by Moses and then, many centuries later, by Nehemiah, it is recorded that all the people answered, "Amen."

Paul assures us that "all the promises of God find their Yes in him. That is why we utter the Amen through him, to the glory of God."

Pondering on the meaning of the word, which really cannot be defined, and feeling its spell upon his spirit, one wrote these lines:

> I heard it all, I heard the whole
> Harmonious hymn of being,
>   roll
> Up through the chapel of
>   my soul
> And at the altar die.
> And in the awful quiet, then,
> Myself, I heard Amen, Amen,
> Amen, I heard me cry.

Somehow in the word "amen" are pledged all the resources of one's utmost might to the service of some idea or cause. It is a personal word, but it is also a national word. History has been made by that to which nations have said "amen." But it can have either a heavenly or a hellish connotation. Blasphemous "amens" have lighted the way to destruction.

Nothing is more significant in this turning point of history, when the blessing or the curse is being chosen by the peoples of the earth, than the answer to the question: "To what is America adding her 'amen'?" The ages to come may be colored by the reply to that interrogation.

The powers of darkness that we fight as we stand at Armageddon have said "amen" to the doctrine that individual man is of value only as the servant, and perhaps the slave, of a police state. America (and those who stand with her in the free world) have said "amen" to the doctrine that man is of supreme value because God created him and endowed him with inalienable rights. Of the two points of view, worlds apart, it can emphatically be said "never the twain shall meet."

An outstanding American religious leader is positively justified in his pronouncement: "One of these systems is going down."

In this world crisis it is of paramount importance to make crystal clear the flaming convictions to which the American "amen" is attached. There is nothing more vital for the future of this planet than the discovery of America by the nations now emerging from exploitative colonialism. It is also vital that in spite of the blandishments of communism they shall see that system for what it is—the most colossal and slavish colonialism the ages have known.

Not in arrogant boasting, which, thank God, has been purged from our American dream, but in humble acceptance of a providential task we can say "amen" to words uttered more than fifty years ago by Senator Albert J. Beveridge: "God's great purposes are being revealed in a manner which surpasses the intentions of Congress and cabinets. We cannot fly from our world duties. It is ours to execute the purpose of a faith that has driven us to be greater than our small intentions."

We have put Kipling's "Recessional" in our hymnals, but

long after it was there the American "amen" was very faint to the words, "Still stands thine ancient sacrifice, an humble and a contrite heart." A spirit of isolation dimmed the poem's stirring words.

But now a chastened and an alerted America, seeing clearly that neighborliness has nothing to do with distance or geography, has learned, please God, the hard lesson that history teaches—namely, that privilege can be a thing with which to commit suicide, and that the only thing to do with strength is to give it away; that any might that does not serve weakness is doomed. No retribution surpasses the penalties of misused strength. Nations whose strength has been stored, instead of poured, have reverted first to weakness and then to oblivion.

One of the heartening signs of the present situation is pointed to in a challenging address by William I. Nichols, former editor of *This Week* magazine. He said: "People are seeking some new sense of dedication, of 'meaningful involvement.' They want to find something above and beyond themselves which will make life important and worth living." That means that America is looking for tremendous commitments to which, with all her vast power, she can say "amen."

Elizabeth Barrett Browning sang America's "amen" in these lines:

> "Happy are all free peoples,
>   too strong to be dispossessed:
> But blessed are those among nations,
>   who dare to be strong for the rest!"

There is the beatitude of America at its best. Blessed is the nation that dares to be strong—for the rest! To measure up to the implications of that supreme role, America must take the pen of her idealism and sign anew for this day of destiny the compact that was in the hands of the Pilgrim fathers as they landed on the wild and bleak New England coast—a compact which began, "In the Name of God, Amen."

The Eloquence of
Silence

EVERY life desperately needs a Chapel of Silence apart from the strife of tongues. The greatest things always are said and heard in the silences, away from great debates which vociferously rend the air with contending voices. The most vital things that any man has to say in public are given to him in brooding hours far from the madding crowd with its loud and distracting accents.

In the silent cocoon the butterfly grows its resplendent wings. Lent is a cloistered enclosure offering the high privilege of listening to the voices of abiding truth symbolized not by the earthquake or whirlwind but by the still small voice.

Jesus knew the creative silences of the hills and the wilderness. Paul's immortal insights on life and death came out of three years of silence apart from the haunts of men.

Silent arguments are the final and effective ones. The unspoken arguments are the unanswerable ones. Truth can afford to wait in quietness and restraint. Fiery verbal missives hurled from the platform or legislative halls, in law courts or over the radio, are answered at last by the truth which, assailed by windy words, abides in silence. It utters no indignant rebuttal but, nevertheless, is eloquent in its ultimate disclosure.

What is said about things is not half as important as what things say about themselves. How often their silent testimony refutes and confronts noisy affirmation about them! For instance, notwithstanding the confident assurance of the defenders of Ussher's chronology, which put the timetable of creation at 4004 B.C., the wise old earth never believed anything of the kind; but it spun on making no audible refutation regarding its alleged age. However, there were uncut leaves in the book of nature, in the coal and chalk beds, on the ocean floors, and in the rocks, all proving that the recent date was not inspired by truth. At last the record was opened and the planet had its say. Always it is the unspoken arguments that finally prevail.

The finest contribution one can bring to the common life is likely to be the precious things apprehended in the experience of aloneness. Solitude is the richest mine for spiritual wealth. It is the most golden part of our inheritance as spiritual beings. Modern life, with its hectic amusements, its grinding traffic, its crowded cities, and its mob movements, seems to be a huge conspiracy against the sacrament of silence and solitude. So low an estimate have men of their own company that any chance to be alone is likely to be avoided. The tendency is to do anything and to go anywhere in order to take our minds off ourselves. The proffered gift of the closet with its closed door is despised. Yet, all the most worthwhile human achievements have come out of solitude. Our utmost inward development awaits our practice of it.

A wise use of the eloquence of silence will teach us how to make solitude a stairway to the highest. The disciplined mind can enter its own secret chapel anywhere, at a moment's notice, where beyond these voices there is peace and meaningful silence.

Tennyson's brother, Frederick, dreaded the chatter of small talk so characteristic of a social reception. The poet laureate was heard to whisper, as together they approached the babble of an afternoon tea, "Frederick, just think of Herschel's star clusters!" It was a plea to escape from social stairs to celestial stars.

A devout Christian businessman living in the suburbs and commuting daily to New York, had to pass through four dark tunnels before reaching his destination. He tells how he made the subway a sanctuary: "When the tunnel is entered you know that in two minutes you will be dumped into the crowded streets. But alone in the dark I have found that the best time to pray I ever discovered. I find I can do real business with God in those two minutes." And so the underground roar became but a fence to guard a rendezvous with the unseen.

Toward the end of his life Thomas Carlyle exclaimed, "I think the happiest of all men is he who can keep himself the quietest." And Cardinal Newman matched that insight when he said, "We are never less alone than when alone."

They were but reechoing Isaiah's rare insight: "in quietness and in trust shall be your strength." Solitude is an enclosed garden where bloom the choicest flowers of grace. The eloquence of the sacramental silence makes it, indeed, the Oratory of the Soul.

John Oxenham's prayer for a little silent place comes with a healing touch for the earthquake and whirlwind of social convulsion. He prays for—

> A solitude where I can think,
> A haven of retreat,
> Where of Thy red wine I may drink
> And of Thy white bread eat.
>
> Come! Occupy my silent place,
> And make Thy dwelling there!
> More grace is wrought in quietness
> Than any is aware.

A Pocket with
Holes

A POCKET is one of the crowning conveniences of civilization. Selfishly filled pockets have long been symbols of the greedy and acquisitive person of whom it is said, "He is always thinking of his own pockets."

There are those who simplify the underlying causes of the social revolution now shaking the earth by declaring that they are essentially contests between the haves and the have-nots; that is, between pockets that are full and pockets that are empty.

Around the world perhaps the most ubiquitous subject of conversation is the United States of America. In our familiar figure of Uncle Sam are centered the hopes and fears of the nations. To many he is a savior; to others he is a gangster. In some places he is canonized; in others he is cannonaded. To some he is a bad Robin Hood with his grasping hands in the pockets of others; to most he is a Good Samaritan bending in mercy and help over the misery of a planet. There are a dozen things about Uncle Sam which, if brought up in the not-so-United Nations, would be the signal for vociferous debate.

But, from under this Spire, where gathers a vast congregation singing from grateful and proud hearts, "God bless America, land that we love," let us consider one item not visible in his beflagged striped costume but yet vital—his pockets!

The most important question constantly before the president, Congress, columnists, and press and magazine editors—the subject of endless disquisitions by learned economists—has to do with the contents of Uncle Sam's pockets. Always the question before the House is: For what purposes and to what extent should the gold coins that jingle there be poured out in response to the multiplied pleadings for the world's woe and the nation's welfare?

When those who represent the fifty states consider budgets and appropriations, they are talking about Uncle Sam's pockets. When the president and congressional leaders warn about inflation and flash red lights outside the dwindling gold reserves in Kentucky, they are anxious about the effect on the Republic's strength if this most affluent nation, even for good causes, pours out more than it takes in. All this is included in what a columnist called "fiscal thinking." Liberals and conservatives agree on one point—there is no subject of study more pertinent than Uncle Sam's pockets.

The Book of books has a very wise thing to say about pockets. One of the old Hebrew prophets bewails the sad fact that man so often toils and then, after receiving monetary compensation for his work, squanders it on things that harm him. The Good Book says of such a man, "He . . . earns wages to put them into a bag [pocket] with holes" (Haggai 1:6). One of the spreading holes that desperate attempts are being made to sew up is called inflation. Everybody loses by that and blessed are the public servants who find the thread to patch these rents before the pockets of the United States turn into disastrous sieves.

What a parable this figure of speech—a pocket with holes—suggests with regard to spiritual losses! For instance, there is the golden thing called time—the most priceless commodity on earth—which so often is wasted on trivialities. If redeemed, that very time could be transmuted into new knowledge, new insights, new skills, new appreciations. But the precious hours that could have made us taller have been prostituted to ignoble uses. A fitting epitaph on the grave of dead hopes, dead resolves, dead ambitions, and dead chances, would be, "He had holes in his pockets."

On a Sunday morning two newlyweds decided to go to hear a good man preach. The messenger was venerable, his benign face an illumined parchment upon which self-denial and devotion had written the radiant story of ripening experiences and revelations. People not only wrote *reverend* before his name —they wrote *revered* after it. Stern discipline through the years had kept him from trading the titanic for the tiny. As that minister leaned over the pulpit, the young couple felt that he was talking just to them. His message might well have been called "Holes in Pockets." He spoke about sowing and reaping. There were two telling sentences that neither of them ever forgot. He said, "Youth should saddle itself with the burden of restraint so that age may never feel the misery of remorse. Youth should take up the burden of achieving so that age may never be crushed beneath a load of shame." He was really pleading that youth should be careful so that there are no holes in life's pockets through which essential things may be lost.

As we face the implications of that piercing truth, it is time for us as Americans to rivet prayerful attention on national fiscal common sense and, guarding against holes in individual pockets—which in the end may make us paupers—to search not only our pockets but our hearts.

Blackberries or a
Burning Bush

In the spring, bushes are aflame with thrilling beauty, and trees, with wardrobe of delicate green, are decked with rainbow ribbons.

It was the resurrection season of the year, when the time for the singing of birds had come, which inspired Elizabeth Barrett Browning to write: "Every common bush [is] afire with God." But she hastened to warn that "only he who sees takes off his shoes." What happens to those who, having eyes, see not a glory which is so near? "The rest," she said, "sit round it and pluck blackberries."

That is not at all to discount the delicious black pyramids that lift their juicy ambrosia with the tantalizing invitation, "First come first served." What the poet means by her reference to burning bushes and blackberries is that to miss the first by exclusive and greedy attention to the second symbolizes life's most devastating tragedy.

George Bernard Shaw remarked that inside every life there are a marketplace and a cathedral. Alas for one whose feet never tread the cloistered sanctuary! What we feel, what we hear, and what we see depend not simply on something in our environment but on something in ourselves. Every one of us owes infinite things to spiritual guides who lead us from the blackberries to the bushes that burn.

In one of his essays, Hazlitt gratefully tells what one walk with the poet Coleridge meant for him. It opened vistas of a totally new world, so near, and yet which had eluded him—a world, too, with far-reaching horizons. That country walk unveiled magic realms of thought and vision of which, until then, he had never dreamed.

So it was with Moses when he heard a voice out of a burning bush. In hot anger he had slain an Egyptian because he was a representative of the tyranny that held his people in bondage. But suddenly out of a common bush that burned and was not consumed, as the future lawgiver turned aside to see this great thing, he heard the summons to be the instrument in God's hand, not to match the brute force of the oppressor, but to bring deliverance for his people by the might of Israel's partnership with invincible spiritual forces.

Without the ear that heard the voice and the eye that marveled at the perpetual light, nothing would have happened except, perhaps, an afternoon siesta for the tired pilgrim. As it was in the beginning, is now, and ever shall be, with the meadow and the moment there must be matched the mood before any wayside bush will be seen to burn with a revelation of God. There were many who had observed apples falling from laden branches in verdant orchards without the thud of ripened fruit on the hard ground suggesting any thoughts higher than apple pie or dumplings, until Isaac Newton saw in their fall the working of the law that upholds the spheres in their orbits and swings the celestial chariots in space.

Some walk in a world where God seems strangely absent simply because they never turn from blackberries long enough to see the burning bushes. We talk about socialism, capitalism, and communism, and the chief things we have in mind may have to do with more efficient cultivation and distribution of the fruits of the good earth. It may all be based on the "blackberry philosophy," a more just arrangement for man's physical needs. But man cannot live by bread alone. Men are not swine, to be provided with bigger and better sties, where food will be made available with the minimum of exertion. The deepest needs of men and women cannot be compassed by material advance.

There is no ultimate salvation of humanity, in all the perplexities and intimacies of living together, without reverences that bow the soul, solemnities that erect altars of worship, and a sense of the eternal that removes dusty sandals on holy ground where bushes burn with God. No Utopia will work which spells man with a capital *M* and God with a small *g*.

While blackberries still grow and need to be picked, burning bushes still blaze and wait to be seen by those who with reverent feet turn aside to see this greatest of all things. When any system makes the state the all-inclusive loyalty, such a finite circle shuts in blackberries, but it shuts out the burning bush. It ignores the primary instinct planted within man's questing spirit that there is something above him: some One above any little social system which will have its day and cease to be, some One above all who temporarily sit in the seats of the mighty, some One that possesses the right to his devout, supreme allegiance. Democracy declares that there is holy ground over which no governmental flag can fly.

Shakespeare rightly called reverence "the angel of the world." Research without reverence for men and nations is a path that leads to futility and frustration.

The Man in the
Mirror

In a store window in our nation's capital a conspicuous placard announced Mirrors for Sale. Now, in all the world there is nothing more vital for any person than to see his own likeness in a looking glass. Such a reflection never tells one the facts about others, but just the brutal truth about himself.

That was why in merry England good Queen Bess got rid of the mirrors in her palace—the royal looking glass told the truth about herself.

There is always one petition in the complete prayer—"Show me myself." It was Tennyson who penned that majestic line, "Be loyal to the royal in yourself."

James put it exactly in the New Testament: "For if any one is a hearer of the word and not a doer, he is like a man who observes his natural face in a mirror; for he observes himself and goes away and at once forgets what he was like."

No wonder that psychiatrists take mirrors in their hands rather than telescopes for those mentally maladjusted who crowd their offices and recline on their couches. These probers of souls complain that one of the chief difficulties is to get their patients to face themselves. Nearly always they dodge the flash of the incriminating mirror.

In a message from an outstanding friend, he reminded his readers, who are a multitude, that in our personal lives we, every one of us, need more hand mirrors. In this letter the writer referred to a well-known American, former Senator Albert W. Hawkes, who some years ago in his valedictory on the floor of the United States Senate quoted some pertinent verses about "The Man in the Glass." The inspiring fact is that in his distinguished career this devoted patriot has, in all kinds of public addresses and by constant personal appeals, from sea to shining sea, sounded forth the trumpet of the gospel of the YOU, as he has worn the white flower of a blameless life.

On National Labor Day 1968 more than fifty eminent citizens from all parts of this land journeyed to the home of this fighter for industrial, commercial, and civil righteousness. The guests were gathered around a glorious replica of the heroic statue of George Washington praying at Valley Forge, recently dedicated on that revered spot by the Freemasons of Pennsylvania at Freedoms Foundation—that rainbow of promise of the Republic where millions of Americans daily cry out, "America, America, God mend thine every flaw." There Dr. Kenneth Wells, president of Freedoms Foundation, repeated the inscription underneath: "Albert W. Hawkes, truly beloved American citizen, who knows more about freedom and equality than any other man of his generation."

The mirror that our own self reflects, keeping its crystal secret well, always asks the questions, "Does life for you center in self or service? Is it a quest for power over your fellows, or on behalf of them?" Napoleon Bonaparte stands for the first passion; Louis Pasteur for the second.

This, then, is our spire of the spirit:

> When you get what you want in your
> struggle for self
> And the world makes you king for
> a day
> Just go to the mirror and look at
> yourself
> And see what that man has to say.
> You may be a Jack Horner and chisel
> a plum
> And think you're a wonderful guy
> But the man in the glass says you're
> only a bum

If you can't look him straight in
the eye.
You may fool the whole world down
the pathway of years
And get pats on the back as you
pass
But your final reward will be
heartaches and tears
If you've cheated the man in the
glass.

In the last analysis we cannot give to the world what we, ourselves, do not have. An adage has come down the long years which is the quintessence of the centuries: "You cannot make a silk purse out of a sow's ear." It was that towering figure in ancient Greece, Socrates, who had as his fundamental principle of life, "Know thyself." Without that you will go in the wrong direction toward vexation and ruin. Always the problem of problems is *you!* That is why Ibsen, the famous dramatist, writing to a young man in whose *you* he was deeply interested, gave the youth this priceless advice: "There is no way by which you can benefit society more than by coining the metal in yourself."

In the marvelous words of George Herbert, "By all means salute thyself—see what thy soul doth wear. Dare to look into thy chest, 'tis thy own!"

When I was last in dear old England, at one twilight I sat alone at the tomb of that loved, prophetic preacher of the unseen, G. A. Studdert-Kennedy. I was not thinking of what we call death, but what he did with life on earth before he went through death to the risen life. Before he passed to that other side, he declared that at the final bar of the Judge of all earth he expected God to ask him just one question, "Well, what did *you* make of it—what did you do with *you?*" What he was saying was that when the Master of all good workmen looked at him staring back from the glass, the only question would be, "What have *you* done with the face in the mirror?"

Putting In
or Taking Out

THE reason that the Dead Sea is dead is that it takes everything in and gives nothing out. It has no outlets. It does nothing to fructify the region around it. That sort of self-centered policy always ends in deadness—in a sea, a person, or a nation.

A modern sage declared that a gentleman is one who puts a little more into the general pool of human welfare than he takes out. In the immortal story usually called "The Prodigal Son," the boy with the wanderlust and the yearning for independent adventure said to his father as he prepared to cut the apron strings of home, "Give me my portion of the family fortune." And he made off with it. After the far country had reduced him to the status of the hogs about him, he finally came to his real self. Then he was anxious and returned home, saying to his father: "Make me a hired servant—I want to make a contribution to the family life I spurned."

There are two attitudes to life—"Give me" and "Make me." The ambition of the first is to store and of the second to pour. The one thinks of life as a selfish storehouse; the other thinks of life as a channel of service to others. The symbol of one is a sponge, which, by the way, is dead. The symbol of the other is a crystal stream, which carpets its banks in verdant green and paints them with flowers.

The most pernicious aspect of our modern day, with its opulent cornucopia of riches in terms of gadgets, comforts, and amusements, is the attitude of multitudes who continually measure their lives by the returns and rewards made to them by people, by society, by government. Certainly, as evidenced by the present-day demand for a paternalistic government, we have raised a generation who think much more of a bill of rights than they do of a bill of responsibilities.

Most success stories, whose subtitle might be "How to Get On in the World," assume that to get on is to "get." Many in the modern race who acquire things run right past the red light of warning waved by Benjamin Franklin, who sagely observed, "Success has ruined many a man." Too often, with "Give me" the ruling passion of life, so-called success in the business and industrial world means to accumulate wealth—by any methods. In government it tends to favor socialistic schemes which kill personal initiative and scorn thrift and frugality.

The give-me philosophy assumes that man is just a mouth to be fed and all that is needed as one steps on the escalator of security is plenty of bread and shortness of hours. In politics the give-me motive means skulduggery in the next election and treachery to the next generation. The ultimate in this "taking out" attitude is suggested by two sentences from the biography of a well-known financier, of whom it was baldly said: "Life to him was just one huge stock exchange and his fellow creatures only so many share-selling, share-buying bipeds. To him dividends meant everything." He might have been a great financier, but he was not a great man.

When he heard of the death of John Calvin, Pope Pius IV remarked, "That heretic's strength lay in the fact that money never had the slightest charm for him." This papal eulogy can be truthfully applied to all who have meant most in humanity's long trek from darkness to light.

Once, in days when America's other name was Opportunity, the national emblem might have been a stairway—a stairway kept open from the bottom to the top—up which any individual could climb who was ready to pay the cost in effort. Of course, it always was inherent in the American conception that those who could not climb, for reasons for which they were not responsible, must be assisted and sometimes carried by the strong, who gladly and gratefully would share and bear the infirmities of the weak. But, alas, now many seem ready to put the stairway to be climbed by personal exertion in the museum of outdated contrivances and to adopt in place of it, as a symbol of American society, a moving escalator which carries all people up automatically, whether they themselves move or not.

There are ominous indications that too many people who belong to the give-me or carry-me group are perfectly willing just to recline on the moving stairs and spend their time looking at the scenery. Life that is geared as an escalator, although conceivably it might get many material things for people, might at the same time do terrible things to people by robbing them of self-respect and a sturdy independence which fosters personal initiative and develops character. Anyone who understands human nature knows that when any system takes away from a man the lure of accomplishment by his own prowess and powers, it is tampering with something very precious—his opinion of himself.

A great English churchman, commenting on the sort of social system a good many Englishmen seemed to think would solve all present ills, made this significant statement: "What is so often forgotten is that if you give endlessly to people who are at heart grabbing and selfish you will bring the life of the community to chaos. Human motives can be poisoned with a drug that steals away the moral grandeur and stamina of the whole land. We might label this drug: 'How can I do less and gain more?' "

Personal responsibility is the central theme of Christianity. One of the fundamental principles of the Master of men was: If a man shall save his life, he shall lose it. That puts life abundant, as Jesus taught it, at the disposal of those whose ruling passion is not "How much can I take out?" but "How much can I put in?" The symbol of all that now, in this desperate day, has made our American democracy mighty enough to be the greatest factor in saving the world from the horror of regimented communism, is not the automatic escalator on which people ride, but the stairway up which people climb.

Praying for Humor

FOR far too long it was assumed that when religion came in the door, humor went out the window. It was that attitude spilling over on canvas that led one modern critic to remark that paintings of most medieval saints make them look as if they were suffering from attacks of acute indigestion. That makes it all the more remarkable that in one of the hoary English cathedrals which so many Americans visit there is hung a framed prayer with the unusual request, "Give me a sense of humor, Lord/grant me the grace to see a joke."

Of course, there are other petitions for other things listed in this versified prayer, such as the gift of daily bread and the digestion to take care of it, a body kept at its best, a healthy mind that keeps the good and pure in sight, a mind that is not bored and does not whimper or whine. Then at the end comes the climax, over which we want to hold a powerful magnifying glass:

> Give me a sense of humor, Lord,
> Grant me the grace to see a joke,
> To get some happiness in life
> And pass it on to other folk.

As one scans the different petitions of this prayer which for so long has adorned the old gray walls of Chester Cathedral, and which one recent traveler declared was the best thing she brought back home, it is apparent that the answers will not come by a divine wand waved without, but from a determined will within. One of the most startling facts of the spiritual life in its practical significance is that the praying one can answer so many of his own prayers. The nearest and most likely channel for answers to the requests we make of Deity is so often through ourselves. The cathedral prayer illustrates that.

Of what avail is it to ask God to give us a pure heart if the walls of our imagination are plastered with obscene pictures? It is of no use to pray for the preservation or restoration of the human body if that body is treated not as a holy temple, but as a filthy sty. Wholeness is always a close neighbor to holiness. But how many there are with their tenement of clay decked out in mink coats or the masculine equivalent, who live and move in a world of boredom.

Boredom is the listless state of mind when the "I" no longer lives with Alice in Wonderland.

But let us underline the appeal for a sense of humor. One who was delighted with the prayer when she read it in the cathedral, remarked as afterward she perused the card on which it was printed, "It's about the only prayer I ever saw or heard which asks God for a sense of humor." But why not? Does not the Bible, which even in Japan is now a best seller, declare, "A cheerful heart is a good medicine"? A heart that is glad and radiant, and songful, is better medicine for certain states of the body than any on the apothecary shelves. Of course we are not thinking of a cheap and perverted humor which snickers at the gross and dances a jig on sacred soil, and wallows gleefully through the rotten, for the sake of a grin.

Perhaps by now someone is saying, here is a world plowed with desolation and gloom and the anxious threat of the devastating split atom, and here is a Spire devoted to an unimportant thing like humor. But wait—well has it been said that God gave us humor to save us from going mad. There are gleams of it in the greatest literature—page Shakespeare! Lincoln declared, "With the fearful strain that is on me night and day, if I did not laugh I should die."

There is a surprising amount of humor in the sayings of Jesus. After worshiping in a certain church a good preacher friend of mine commented, "Sometimes when I hear the lessons read so solemnly in church, I see in imagination Peter and John in the back pew. They seem to nudge each other and say, 'He wouldn't read like that if he had heard the Master talking.'"

The record does not say Jesus laughed, because he laughed so often, but once when tears glistened it says, "Jesus wept."

When one who loves humor saw how much of it was in Jesus' picture of the fat old Pharisee drinking soup, straining out a gnat and swallowing a camel, he suggested—shut your eyes and imagine a camel going down! And this is but one of many places where the smile wrinkles are about Jesus' eyes. Wasn't it the most discounting thing they could say of the Man of Galilee that he was a habitual partygoer and his companions publicans and sinners?

Shall we say that *The Music Man,* so saturated with good humor, is worth more than dozens of lugubrious sermons on "sinners in the hands of an angry God"?

One of the saintliest men I ever knew—a great teacher and preacher—lived always in an atmosphere of droll wit. When he lay dying, and those around thought he was unconscious, a nurse feeling his feet said, "They're still warm and no one ever dies with warm feet." The good doctor, only a few hours from his death, opened his eyes and with a smile so true to form said (as he thought of the flames around the feet of a famous martyr), "Yes, John Huss did."

That scene seems to fit the suggestion of a present-day teacher and preacher known around the world: "Let us, like the cat in Alice in Wonderland, resolve that the grin shall be the last thing to vanish," praying always for a sense of humor and the grace to laugh at a joke.

If He
Had Not Come

IN THE GLOW and glory of Christmastide, to a well-known preacher there came a dream, dark and dismal. The disturbing fantasy was in such sharp contrast to the radiant reality of which he was a herald that, on awakening, the dreamer ever afterward lived in thankful exultation that his experience was just a horrible nightmare.

As the preacher sat quietly in his study by blazing logs, he found himself turning almost automatically to a chapter in the New Testament that he really knew by heart. Suddenly there flashed out a phrase not noticed before: "If I had not come. . . ." That awful possibility had never been contemplated. He read no farther. That *if* gripped him like a vise. The cheery room seemed suddenly to grow cold. The New Testament dropped to his knees, and he began to dream of a Christless world, a world into which the Child of the manger had not come.

Walking through city streets on the 25th of December, peering into homes, the preacher saw no signs that those who had much were caring for the underprivileged. Sick at heart, he remembered with a shudder that he was in a world into which the Christ had not come. Then, in his dream, he turned his steps homeward, but came to a sudden pause as he looked with astonishment. On one side of the street was a great gap in the row of buildings. He was bewildered by the vacant place. Without question, that was where his own church, St. Peter's, used to stand; but it was there no longer. He looked up to the crest of the hill, where the great cathedral had risen in Gothic majesty. The height was desolate and bare. Every steeple and spire had gone from the city skyline. He held his breath in panic and anguish as the devastating thought came flooding that this was an earth to which Christ had not come. Nor was that all! Other buildings had disappeared—the hospital and the home for the aged and the orphanage had been wiped out of the picture. But not the prison; that was there, in all its forbidding ugliness. What a pitiless world!

Finally, with a sigh of relief, he escaped from the streets into the quiet of his own home and study. But quickly he found that shocking surprises were by no means at an end. The honored shelf where he kept his prized lives of Christ was bare. Again, he remembered this was a world to which Christ had not come. And here was the special poets' corner, where were grouped the masters of the human spirit, whose spiritual insights had been his meat and drink. The books were all there, and the titles seemed to be saying, "Do yourself no harm; we are all here." There they were—Shakespeare, Milton, Tennyson, Browning.

Rejoicing that the works of that preacher's poet, Browning, were still intact, he eagerly picked up the volume and fingered through the familiar pages. What he found made him start with astonishment. There were appreciative annotations on the margins; but, again and again, in the center of the page was but a blank space. It was as if some vandal had effaced the finest passages. Quickly, and with dread, he opened his Shakespeare. The destroyer had been at work there also. He snatched up Tennyson. Only fragments of the matchless "In Memoriam" were left. Milton he found mangled beyond recognition.

Disconsolately sitting down before the wreck of his loved books, the preacher tried to puzzle out what had happened. Of course, he remembered that the beginning of "In Memoriam," which was missing, was: "Strong Son of God, immortal Love." Here was the clue. He found that every line in the poems about Christ, or inspired by Christ, had disappeared. He was in a world in which the noblest half of his literature had vanished, because Christ had not come. Even the ritual, which he had taken so confidently into sickrooms and read with triumphant assurance at open graves, was in tatters. There was no

Christ; therefore, there was no: "Let not your hearts be troubled. . . . In my Father's house are many rooms. . . . Because I live, you will live also."

Then, in the tragedy and pathos of such a world, with a great sob clutching his throat, he awoke to find this cruel, pitiless, Christless world was only a dream. He could plainly hear the choir in the nearby church singing the wondrous words: "Joy to the world! the Lord is come." It had all been only a dream, an ugly, hideous dream; but it taught him to appreciate as never before the ineffable gift bestowed upon our race at Bethlehem.

Here is the grateful testimony of the dreamer: "Never did I know how much the world owed to Jesus Christ until I dreamed of the world to which he had never come. The vision of that world without a CHRISTMAS, without a church, without a cross—the vision of that world without pity and without heart—the vision of that world in which life was misery and death despair, brought to my heart a new Te Deum because I lived in a world into which Christ had come. It was then that I realized that pity and sympathy and love and hope, the things that make life glad and beautiful, were born with Christ at Bethlehem."

Everybody's
Saint

THERE is, perhaps, only one picture that fits the frame of "everybody's saint." It is the likeness of Saint Francis of Assisi. He lived out his brief span twelve hundred years after the sandaled feet of the Master he adored trod the dusty ways of Galilee. In the radiant personality of Francis the very spirit of the Nazarene was so incarnated that its incandescence has illumined the succeeding ages.

In his life was fulfilled the definition given by a wee maiden who was asked to answer the profound adult question, "What is a saint?" She had been told that the figure portrayed in the jeweled glass of a window near where she sat in church with her parents was that of a saint, and often she had watched the sunlight stream through it. Her reply to the query was beautifully accurate. "A saint," she said, "is somebody the light shines through."

The light of the world so shone through Saint Francis that everything else said about that human window seems utterly irrelevant. The one glorious fact is that in the life of this poor man of Assisi the light shines through. Now, as when under Italian skies he was a brother to all the sons of men, it is true that the people who walk in darkness have seen a great light because of one man who really never has died. He belongs to the ages and to the Christ of the ages.

No wonder that in the capital city of our nation one of the most significant magnets, drawing by a mystic attraction multitudes of pilgrims of every religion, is the monastery and basilica that bears his revered name. There under the open heavens his sculptured form seems transformed to flesh before understanding eyes. There the little chapel, so simple and crude, which speaks of his trysting place with God, becomes a cathedral of the seeking spirit. Somehow in the cloistered loveliness of this gardened enclosure, shut off from the world's busy traffic, Catholic and Protestant, and even devotees of other faiths, feel alike the spell of this humble monk.

Saint Francis has inspired uncounted millions by revealing that a single individual entirely given to the Holy One, whose life is light, can become a flaming beacon of everlasting mercy. In the home of a Protestant clergyman there recently was seen a perfectly charming representation of "everybody's saint" standing with appealing grace in the midst of a miniature garden, surrounded by his loved feathered comrades.

"That is a constant inspiration to us all," said the preacher. "In our home it has become an altar where in this grasping day we hear his gentle rebuke for all self-seeking. The beauty of holiness streams through the saint of the universal church whom we have taken to our hearts and who really lives in our home."

With one voice those who are keenly aware of spiritual realities quite apart from all dogma and ceremony would give Rufus Jones, the Quaker, a place among the chief twelve of Christ's disciples in this twentieth century. Shall we ask this prophetic sage what "everybody's saint" meant to him? Quickly and eagerly he replies:

It was from St. Francis of Assisi that I learned the infinite importance of gentleness, humility, simplicity and tenderness. There seems to be in this God's poor little man a spontaneity of joy and wonder that is like a fresh stream of life bursting forth from the immortal font of life itself. Religion in him changes from debate and argument, from doctrine and system, from calculation and utility schemes, to a sheer thrill and burst of joyous life and love.

Who that has read the story of the Christian centuries does not love Saint Francis? And why? It is the man's gallant joyfulness that grips you, the joy that sang its way in beggar's clothes around Italy, earning for him that blithesome and most honorable name, God's troubadour. The joy leaped like fire from his soul to a thousand others, until tens of thousands had been kindled at its torch and a dead church, feeling that the winter was past and that the time for the singing of birds had come, broke from its sleep in sudden resurrection.

And so, on Christmas Day comes a moving advent greeting from "everybody's saint," Francis of Assisi, who perhaps as no other mortal reenacted the Incarnation in his own life.

More than twelve hundred years after the Bethlehem manger he stood with his hand lifted, as he stands in so many statues and pictures across the centuries, and always above him is a burst of birds singing—and beyond him is the break of dawn.

Saint Francis still breathes his eternal prayer which, when practiced, brings Christmas everywhere!

Thunder and the
Angels

THUNDER, with its ominous rumblings and its sudden, fearsome explosions, is often one of childhood's most terrifying memories. And back there, in the heaven that lies around those early unspoiled years, angels, although not as audible, were as real as thunder which bombarded the shrinking senses.

In early petitions the prayer was lisped that angels might guard our beds. And, at church, with utter assurance as if their snowy pinions were hovering near, we sang about "angels of light, singing to welcome the pilgrims of the night." But, unfortunately, although thunder crashes still continue to assail the ear with their booming assertions of reality, as years lengthen angel forms tend to become fainter as childish things are put away. Angel guardians become as futile and "frail as frost landscapes on a windowpane."

We can understand and explain thunder; its effects can even be reproduced in a laboratory. But as for the presence and voices of angels, all such conceptions belong to the realm of fairies or of Alice in Wonderland. So a materialistic age has been telling us. We have been living through a time when materialists have gone out on a veritable crusade to debunk the invisible. Readily they have agreed to analyze the phenomenon of a thunderstorm, but, disdainfully, angels have been ignored. They have been so engrossed with scientific progress that they have actually lost the faculty of seeing or sensing anything else. These denizens of the seen hear the whirl of machinery, the deafening roar of human traffic, and the thunder of global contentions. All that is obvious and audible. But angels—they belong to hymns and stained-glass windows, and not to any universe an intelligent modern can know anything about.

But once, when the most spiritually sensitive Person who ever trod this earth was conscious of voices from the outside reaching his soul, in tune with the Infinite, some persons nearby with no receiving sets heard only ordinary earthly sounds. The record of that epochal day is: "[Some] standing by heard it and said that it had thundered. Others said, 'An angel has spoken to him.'" Some—others. The "some" shrugged their shoulders at those who so naïvely thought the Teacher of Galilee had heard spiritual voices and, with the crass cynicism of a typical materialistic outlook, insisted, "It is nothing but thunder—simply that, and nothing more." There they stand: Some —others.

So it was. And so it is. Thus, men and women stood divided about the Christ twenty centuries ago, as darkened clouds floated across the bending blue of that eastern sky; so they stand today. To some, the world is a great whispering gallery, and everywhere there are voices divine. To others, there are no voices, simply noises. In the clouds of time and sense there are just collisions of physical elements, going it blind; and, in human relationships, only the harsh mutterings of evil passions and selfish ambitions. The better angels of human nature are nowhere to be seen. Thunder represents the final word of the universe. As a newspaper reporter summing up this philosophy of thunder put it: "We have come through the pagan '20s, the depressing '30s, the warring '40s, the A-bomb '50s, and on into the nuclear '60s."

Out of these upheavals is emerging a multiplying number of puzzled humans, asking with a new poignancy, "What does life really mean?" There is a growing realization among frustrated and disillusioned people that the tangibles are about exhausted, and that they have led to futility. These people see now that progress is not an escalator, that expanding knowledge does not always lead to abundant life. It may lead to hell. That the harnessed secrets of nature form no stairway to the Utopia we thought they would, and that boasted know-how does not lead to know-why, is now perfectly clear. Explaining thunder does not explain life. It is increasingly evident that there is something else in life's equation besides thunder. After all, may it not be that there are angels? Which means there is God!

Surely there is more to this mystic experience that stretches across the isthmus from cradle to grave than meets the eye or ear. There is more than Theodore Dreiser found. Hearing only the thunder of what he called "clownish and ridiculous interests," he said, at the last, "I catch no meaning from all I have seen, and pass quite as I came, confused and dismayed."

Majestic faith has to do not with thunder but with angels. The storm clouds, black with muttering wrath, pass. The thunder of Calvary had died to silence when angel forms at an empty tomb hailed the radiant Life a cross could not stop!

> Angels, sing on. Your faithful
> watches keeping,
> Sing as sweet fragments of the
> songs above,
> Till morning's joys shall end
> the night of weeping
> And life's long shadows break
> in cloudless love.

The Wings of the Morning

In historic Wesley's Chapel, London, often I have gazed at a jeweled window, rich in color and symbolism, a gift of devotion from one in faraway Australia. When on wings of the dawn, the westering day, fading from the east, gilds English skies, I have read in that pictured glass this flaming text:

> If I take the wings of the morning
>   and dwell in the uttermost parts of the sea,
>   even there thy hand shall lead me,
>   and thy right hand shall hold me.

Ah, if I had wings, this sojourner so far from home was saying. If I had wings, echoes David's voice across the long centuries!

How beautiful that at dawn God wakes the sleeping earth with the carol of feathered songsters and with the rustling wings of the morning. Wings of the morning! Long has that phrase haunted me. It is not, like some phrases, a pointed shaft to stab a complacent spirit wide awake. It haunts one for the sheer poetry and beauty of it, like moonlight on the sea, like a redbird on a winter bough, or a church spire against a twilight sky—wings of the morning! It is a wedding certificate of two glories that God has joined together, wings and morning.

Wings speak of release from the earthy, emancipation from the ground; kinship with the clouds, the stars, the sky. Morning is dew-pearled, rose-tinted, fleeing shadows, purpling east, songbird answering song from topmost bough in the solemn hush of nature newly born. The phrase is a poem, a picture, and a parable. For wings are symbols of the pinions awaiting every one of us, if we will but claim and use them, to lift a new vision, new strength, new tasks, new achievements, and new victories.

Out of the wonderful drama of Job there comes this question: "Have you commanded the morning . . .?" There could be no more important query than that. If we are not the captain of our soul and our body, then, if the morning mutinies, we are literally doomed to disappointment, failure, and loss. Have you commanded the morning, or does it command you?

One of the most exclusively beautiful sentences in the collection of noble, soul-fathoming Hebrew poetry that we call the Psalms has to do with wings of the morning. On the flat roofs of the houses of Palestine are often found junk piles of discarded household articles, especially pots and pans. Among these rusted vessels doves take refuge during the intense heat of midday. But in the morning and in the evening they leave their sordid refuge for the wide freedom of the cool air and the sky. To the writer of one of the Psalms the rising sun, with its riotous beauty, made the spreading wings of the doves gleam like silver and gold. And so the promise of that ancient paean is, "Though ye have lien among the pots, yet shall ye be as the wings of a dove covered with silver, and her feathers with yellow gold" (KJV). That is a promise that even though common tasks and trivialities may cast our lots on lowly levels, there are wings of the morning which give beauty for ashes and gleaming gold and glistening silver for the black soot of pots and pans.

It matters not how menial your task may be; it matters not what foul forms have peopled your night, "black as the pit from pole to pole"; it matters not what devastating sorrow may have swept across your life or what treasures moth and rust may have corrupted or thieves may have stolen—every new morning brings new wings to fly on to beckoning heights. That is the message of wings and the morning that today we would lift as high as the Spires of the Spirit!

Yesterday is for gratitude and, perhaps, for regret. Today is for resolution and a new start. When morning gilds the skies, it is heaven's signal to reach for your wings—not wearily to tie on old weights. Listen to the Third Psalm:

> O LORD, how many are my foes!
> Many are rising against me;
>
> . . . .
>
> I lie down and sleep;
> I wake again, for the LORD
> sustains me.
> I am not afraid of ten thousands
> of people
> who have set themselves against
> me round about.

In the morning, after a good night's sleep, the psalmist found that his weights had changed to wings.

As soon as we have permitted the past to assert an arresting mastery over us, whether it be the deadening complacency of splendid achievement or the disabling remembrance of dismal failure, we doom ourselves to the ground; we reject the wings of the morning. Of course, only the fool ignores the past. But the man who is governed by his yesterdays is a prisoner, though he may not know it. The accumulated weight of all the yesterdays will crush the wings which otherwise will lift you above it all for a new start and a new day. At sunrise, every soul is born anew. Each morning gives the wings to fly from all that is of the earth, for—

> Every day is a fresh beginning;
> Listen, my soul, to the glad refrain,
> And, spite of old sorrow and older sinning,
> And puzzles forecasted and possible pain,
> Take heart with the day, and begin again.

Wings wait with the morning!

The Beliefs of
Unbelief

THE burden of belief, as it is intellectually and spiritually accepted, has been the frequent theme of thinkers facing the total mystery of life. The beliefs of belief have been stressed in many a dusty tome endeavoring to buttress accepted premises by an apology meant to sugarcoat something otherwise hard to swallow. Such defense of the faith rightly points out that to trust in what are called "spiritual verities" is no easy achievement, and that belief is beset by perils.

Sometimes the impression is given that if the yoke of belief is cast aside the disbeliever is then scot-free of further concern; he is emancipated. There could be no crueler fallacy, for a skeptic faces the beliefs of unbelief. Gazing at the blank and meaningless universe, any intelligent doubter finds himself facing difficulties harder than before.

Of course, there always are those with borrowed creeds who, tongue in cheek, simply say, "It is impossible. Therefore I believe." Even that position is not as far-fetched as it sounds. In many realms faith has demolished so many alleged impossibilities that that word is seen often to be the mask of an impostor. The men who have driven away the specter of the impossible, barring advancing civilization, were great believers. They have been pioneers, like Pasteur, who, in spite of the stare of the wise and the derision of experts, steadfastly proclaimed their faith.

Faith is adventure. Negation is stagnation. The next step in human progress always is an invasion beyond the fences of the impossible.

It is true that a great and compelling faith often walks a

thorny pathway. Any man who jauntily says that he believes in God does not know the tremendous implications of that faith. It is a stupendous affirmation to be made reverently and discreetly and in the fear of the Almighty. The great believers are those who, realizing the difficulty of believing that God is love, have found it harder still to disbelieve. To stand in the presence of some burning bush of beauty or of nobility, of goodness and devotion, and then to say, "I believe all that is just the accidental consequence of colliding atoms, without any root in eternal truth," puts a great weight on credulity. Professor Montague remarked regarding a creed of negation, "The chance of the assumptions of unbelief being true would have to be represented by a fraction with one for a numerator and with a denominator that would reach from here to one of the fixed stars."

To be sure, belief is difficult. But what about the alternative —unbelief? Newman Smyth exclaimed, as he honestly examined unbelief, "How many things hard to credit one must believe in order not to be a Christian!" To be sure, it is doubt which "goes sounding on its dim and perilous way." Unbelief is no lotus-eater's paradise, delightfully free from uncomfortable moral responsibilities. The trouble is that the difficulties of religion are examined under a microscope, but the owner of the microscope does not apply it to his doubts or to the implications of his lack of faith.

The fact is that unbelief itself is a creed with its own unconscious affirmations. The baneful results of blasphemous denials on a tremendous scale already are being shown by the dreadful social pattern of atheistic materialism.

One goes but a little distance along the pathway of deliberate doubt when the suspicion begins to grow that it is not the believer who is irrational, but the cynical denier.

What, then, is the belief of unbelief? It is that souls which have shone with the radiance of faith and hope and love, of honor and valor and self-sacrifice, can be explained by physical or psychological reaction. It is to believe that even a modern Francis of Assisi can be finished irrevocably and forever by a microbe, by a bullet, or by a drunken driver's unbalanced senses. The unbeliever has to assert that the grandeur and glory of life at its highest and best is just the product of blind chance.

No wonder a great thinker analyzing the beliefs of unbelief said: "To me it is all as sensible as declaring that you could take a bag containing the letters of the alphabet and, throwing a few handfuls of them up into the air, expect them to fall to the ground in the form of a Shakespeare's sonnet or of Tennyson's 'In Memoriam.' The thing is absurd."

> There is no unbelief;
> Whoever plants a seed beneath the sod
> And waits to see it push away the clod,
> He trusts in God.
>
> .   .   .   .
>
> There is no unbelief;
> For thus by day and night unconsciously
> The heart lives by the faith the lips deny.
> God knoweth why.